Series 63

Uniform Securities Agent State Law Exam

License Exam Manual
20th Edition

Dearborn
PASSTRAK™

Dearborn

At press time, this edition contains the most complete and accurate information currently available. Owing to the nature of license examinations, however, information may have been added recently to the actual test that does not appear in this edition. Please contact the publisher to verify that you have the most current edition.

This publication is designed to provide accurate and authoritative information in regard to the subject matter covered. It is sold with the understanding that the publisher is not engaged in rendering legal, accounting, or other professional services. If legal advice or other expert assistance is required, the services of a competent professional should be sought.

To submit comments or suggestions, please send an email to errata@dearborn.com.

SERIES 63 UNIFORM SECURITIES AGENT STATE LAW EXAM, LICENSE EXAM MANUAL, 20TH EDITION ©2004 DF Institute, Inc. All rights reserved.

Published by DF Institute, Inc.

Printed in the United States of America.

ISBN: 1-4195-0087-2

PPN: 3663-0120

04	05	10	9	8	7	6	5	4	3	2	1
J	F	M	A	M	J	J	A	S	O	**N**	D

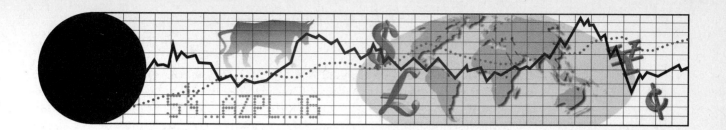

Contents

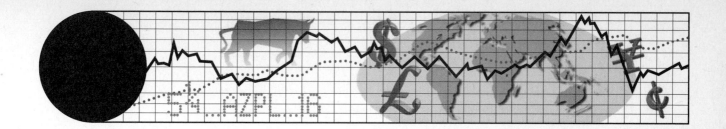

Series 63 Introduction

Thank you for choosing Dearborn's PASSTRAK exam preparation system for your educational needs and welcome to the Series 63 License Exam Manual. This system has been designed with applied adult learning principles to give you the tools you'll need to pass your exam on the first attempt.

Some of these special features include:

- exam-focused questions and content to maximize test preparation;
- an interactive design for the License Exam Manual that integrates content with questions to increase retention; and
- Drill & Practice exam preparation tools to sharpen test-taking skills.

Is there someone I can contact if I have questions as I study?

Dearborn is here to help you with every step of your study process. If you have questions about your study materials, please contact Dearborn's **AnswerPhone** at:

1-800-621-9621 x3598

between 8:00 am and 6:00 pm CT, Monday through Friday. AnswerPhone's staff of content experts will answer your questions and clarify the material as needed. If your inquiry is regarding a particular question in the Practice Final Exams or in the Drill & Practice, please note the QID number (Question Identifier) as this will allow us to find your question within our testing database.

How is the License Exam Manual organized?

Dearborn's *Series 63 License Exam Manual* consists of Units, Unit Exams, and Practice Final Exams. When an additional point will be valuable to your comprehension, special notes are embedded in the text.

✓ ***For Example:*** These provide situations and numerical instances of the material to illustrate a point for increased comprehension of difficult or technical material.

✓ ***Take Note:*** These are tips and commentary that amplify important or unique points.

Test Topic Alert!

Test Topic Alerts highlight content that is likely to appear on the Series 63 exam.

As you read each Unit, you will also see **Quick Quizzes,** which will help you understand and retain the material covered in that particular section. Quick Quizzes are a brief interactive review of what you just read.

In addition, **Unit HotSheets** at the end of each unit summarize the key points in bullet-point format. For your convenience and use as review notes, Hot-Sheets are duplicated at the end of the License Exam Manual on perforated pages.

How is the book organized?

The book is made up of Units outlined in the same way that the North American Securities Administrators Association (NASAA) has outlined the material for the exam.

- Unit 1: Registration of Persons (18 questions, or 30%)
- Unit 2: Securities (15 questions, or 25%)
- Unit 3: Unethical Business Practices (21 questions, or 35%)
- Unit 4: Administrative Provisions of the Uniform Securities Act (6 questions, or 10%)
- Appendix A: Federal Securities Laws
- Appendix B: NASAA's Statements of Policy on Dishonest or Unethical Business Practices by Broker/Dealers, Agents and Investment Advisers

A set of Practice Finals complements the Units presented in the License Exam Manual.

Preparing for the Exam

How much time should I spend studying?

Plan to spend approximately 20 to 30 hours reading the material and working through the questions. Devote a significant amount of your study time to the Practice Finals and review of rationales. Your actual time, of course, may vary from this figure depending on your reading rate, comprehension, professional background, and study environment.

Spread your study time over the two to three weeks before the date on which you are scheduled to take the Series 63 exam. Select a time and place for studying that will allow you to concentrate your full attention on the material. Be sure to give yourself enough time to learn the material—and then test your retention by taking the Practice Finals.

What is the best way to organize my study time?

The following method is suggested to help you obtain maximum retention from your study efforts. Remember, this is intended as a *guideline only*; each individual may require more or less time to complete the steps.

For the License Exam Manual: As you read through each Unit, pause to complete each Quick Quiz and be sure to complete the Unit Exam at the end. Review rationales for all questions whether you scored them right or wrong. In many cases, the rationales bring in additional information relevant to the test.

 Take Note: Do not be overly concerned with your score on the first attempt at any exam. Instead, take the opportunity to learn from your mistakes.

Repeat the above two steps for each unit until you have completed all of the Units in the workbook (2–4 hours per unit). Then direct your attention to the corresponding HotSheet to remind yourself of the points that are highlighted for you. The last step is to complete all of the Practice Finals. Give yourself enough time to take a complete 60-question exam in one sitting (8-10 hours for all exams).

For the CD-ROM: If your study materials include the Series 63 Drill & Practice, this Dearborn CD-ROM includes a large bank of questions that are similar in style and content to those you will encounter on the exam. You can use it to generate exams by specific topic or to create practice finals that are similar in difficulty and topic proportion to the actual Series 63 exam.

On the CD-ROM, create and complete an exam for each topic included under each Unit heading. For best results, select the maximum number of questions within each topic. Carefully review all rationales. Do an additional exam on any topic on which you score under 60%. After you have completed all unit exams, create a 60-question exam comprised of all Unit topics. Repeat this 60-question exam until you score at least 70% (5–10 hours).

Complete at least five of the 60-question Practice Finals. Complete more exams as necessary to achieve a score of at least 80–90%. Create and complete additional topic exams as necessary to correct problem areas (10–20 hours).

Do I need to take all of the exams?

The Practice Finals test the same knowledge you will need to answer the questions on the Series 63 exam. By completing all the exams and checking your answers against the rationale, you should be able to pinpoint areas you are still having difficulty with. Review questions you miss, paying particular attention to the rationale for those questions.

Another important reason to take all of the exams is that we frequently introduce new material using the question format. You will occasionally notice a question covering material unfamiliar to you. Don't worry. Do the question, study the rationale, and you will be ready for the real exam.

If a subject still seems troublesome, go back and review the section covering that topic. It is critical that you understand as much of the material as you can. Merely memorizing questions and answers will not get you a passing grade.

The Series 63 Exam

Why do I need to pass the Series 63 exam?

State securities laws require individuals to pass a qualification exam in order to sell securities within their states.

✓ **Take Note:** Almost all states require representatives to pass the Series 63 exam (blue-sky test) as a condition of state registration.

What is the Series 63 exam like?

The Series 63 is a 75-minute, 60-question exam administered by the NASD. It is offered as a computer-based test at testing sites around the country. A pencil-and-paper exam is available to candidates who get permission from the NASD to take a written exam. There will be five extra questions (for a total of 65 questions) but these five questions are experimental testing questions that do not count against your score. These experimental questions are not identified as such.

Which topics will I see covered on the exam?

The Series 63 exam is divided into four areas. Dearborn's License Exam Manual has four Units, outlined the same way the North American Securities Administrators Association (NASAA) has outlined the material for the exam. This course will take you through the topic areas that the NASAA has outlined as essential to the Series 63 Uniform Securities Agent's exam.

What score must I achieve to pass?

You must answer correctly at least 70% of the questions on the Series 63 exam to pass and become eligible for registration.

How long does the exam take?

You are allowed 75 minutes to finish the exam. If you are taking the computerized version, you will be given additional time before the test—up to half an hour—to take the computer exam tutorial and become familiar with the terminal.

How do I enroll for the exam?

To obtain an admission ticket to the Series 63 exam, your firm must file an application form and fees with the NASD. The NASD will then send you a directory of Prometric Centers and an enrollment valid for a stated number of days. To take the exam during this period, you must make an appointment with a Prometric Center as far in advance as possible of the date on which you would like to sit for the test.

You can contact a Prometric Center at 1-800-578-6273.

What should I take to the exam?

Take one form of personal identification that bears your signature and photograph as issued by a government agency. You cannot take reference materials or anything else into the testing area. Calculators are available upon request; you cannot use a personal calculator. Scratch paper and pencils will be provided by the testing center, although you will not be permitted to take them with you when you leave.

How is the exam administered?

The Series 63 exam, like many professional licensing examinations, is administered on a nationwide, interactive computer system designed for the administration and delivery of qualifications examinations. Included with your enrollment is a brochure describing how the exam is formatted as well as how to use the computer terminal to answer the questions.

When you have completed the exam, the system scores your answers and displays your grade for the exam on the terminal screen.

How well can I expect to do on the exam?

The examination is not easy. You will be required to display considerable understanding and knowledge of the topics presented in this course in order to pass the Series 63 exam and qualify for registration. If you study and complete all of the sections of the course, and score at least 85% on your first attempt on the exams, and, more importantly, understand why the correct answers are correct, you should be well prepared to pass the Series 63 exam. If you repeat the practice exams several times and score in the 85% range, do not conclude that you are fully prepared unless you also understand the concepts the exams are testing. Recognizing answers on repeated questions does not mean you understand the material.

Successful Test-Taking Tips

Passing any NASD Series exam depends not only on how well you learn the subject matter, but also on how well you take tests. You can develop your test-taking skills (and improve your score) by learning a few techniques:

- Read the full question
- Avoid jumping to conclusions—watch for hedge clauses
- Interpret the unfamiliar question
- Look for key words and phrases
- Identify the intent of the question
- Recognize synonymous terms
- Eliminate/short-list Roman numeral choices
- Use a calculator

- Beware of changing answers
- Pace yourself

Each of these pointers is explained below, including examples that show how to use them to improve performance on the NASD exams.

Note: The examples below are not specific to the Series 63 exam.

Read the full question

You can't expect to answer a question correctly if you don't know what it is asking. If you see a question that seems familiar and easy, you might anticipate the answer and move on before you finish reading it. This is a serious mistake. Be sure to read the full question before answering—questions are often written to trap people who assume too much. Here is an example of how a quick assumption can produce a wrong answer.

1. What is the term for a divided underwriting of securities that is priced through a bidding process involving more than one investment banking firm?

    A. Eastern
    B. Western
    C. Negotiated
    D. Competitive

1. **D.** *The answer is D—the question describes a situation in which competitive bidding determines the offering price.*

This is an easy question to answer only for someone who has read the full question, because the point is made in the second half. If you read the question too quickly, you might get to the word *divided* and assume that you are being asked to remember whether a divided underwriting is called an Eastern or Western underwriting.

Avoid jumping to conclusions—watch for hedge clauses

The questions on NASD exams are often embellished with deceptive distractors as choices. To avoid being taken in by seemingly obvious answers, make it a practice to read each question and each answer choice twice before selecting your choice. Doing so will provide you with a better chance of doing well on the test.

Watch out for hedge clauses embedded in the question. Examples of hedge clauses include the terms *if, not, all, none,* and *except.* In the case of *if* statements, the question can only be answered correctly by taking into account the qualifier. If you ignore the qualifier, you will not answer correctly. Qualifiers are sometimes combined in a question. You will frequently see *all* with *except* and *none* with *except.* In general, when a question starts with *all* or *none* and ends with *except,* you are looking for an answer that is opposite to what the question appears to be asking.

2. All of the following are characteristics of Treasury bills EXCEPT that they

    I.   mature in more than one year
    II. are sold at a discount
    III. pay interest semiannually
    IV. are very safe investments

    A. I and II
    B. I and III
    C. II and III
    D. II and IV

2. ***B***. *If you neglect to read the "except," you will look for the choices that are characteristics of T-bills. In fact, the question asks which choices are NOT characteristics of T-bills. T-bills mature in one year or less and do not pay periodic interest; therefore, choices (I) and (III) are incorrect.*

Interpret the unfamiliar question Do not be surprised if some questions on the test seem unfamiliar at first. If you have studied your material, you should have the information to answer all the questions correctly. The challenge may be a matter of understanding what the question is asking. Very often, questions present information indirectly and you have to interpret the meaning of certain elements before you can answer the question. The following two examples concerning bond yields and prices highlight this point:

3. What is the effect of a decline in purchasing power on the current yields of outstanding bonds?

    A. The yields decrease.
    B. The yields increase.
    C. The yields stay the same.
    D. This cannot be determined with the information given.

3. ***B***. *This question is asking you to apply knowledge of economics, investment recommendations, and the relationship between bond prices and yields. Consumer purchasing power declines during periods of inflation. Inflation causes interest rates to rise, and this in turn causes prices of outstanding bonds to decrease. When a bond declines in price or sells at a discount, the current yield increases (B).*

This same content could have been tested in a different way, as illustrated by the next example.

4. What is the effect of tight money on bond prices?

    A. Bond prices decrease.
    B. Bond prices increase.
    C. Bond prices stay the same.
    D. This cannot be determined with the information given.

4. **A**. *Tight money is closely related to high interest rates. When money is scarce (tight), interest rates rise. When interest rates rise, prices of outstanding bonds decrease (A).*

At first glance, the two questions appear very different, but in fact they test the same relationship—the relationship between a bond's price and its yield. Be aware that the exam may approach a concept from different angles.

Look for key words and phrases   Look for words that are clues to the situation presented. For example, if you see the word "prospectus" in the question stem, you know the question is about a new issue. Sometimes a question will even supply you with the answer if you can recognize the key words it contains. The following is an example of how a key word can help you answer correctly:

5. Whose Social Security number must appear on an account under the Uniform Gifts to Minors Act?

   A. Minor
   B. Donor
   C. Legal guardian
   D. Parent

5. **A**. *Looking at the answers, choice A seems a likely candidate. Under UGMA, the minor is the owner of the securities. As the owner, the minor's Social Security number must be listed on the account. Few questions provide clues as blatant as this one, but many do offer key words that can guide you to selecting the correct answer—if you pay attention.*

Be sure to read all instructional phrases carefully, as illustrated in the next example.

6. Rank the following persons in descending order of their claims against a corporation's assets when the corporation is forced into liquidation.

   I.   General creditors
   II. Preferred stockholders
   III. Bondholders
   IV. Common stockholders

   A. I, II, III, IV
   B. I, III, II, IV
   C. III, I, II, IV
   D. III, II, IV, I

6. **C**. *The most important aspect of this question is identifying the key word—descending. A descending order ranks a list from highest to lowest; in this question, the highest claim on assets to the lowest claim on assets. (The answer is C: bondholders, general creditors, preferred stockholders, common stockholders.) The question could have asked for the ascending order—lowest to highest. Or it could have asked you to rank the choices from junior claim to senior claim or vice versa.*

Take time to identify the key words to answer this type of question correctly.

Identify the intent of the question

Many questions on NASD exams supply so much information that it is easy to lose track of what is being asked. Learn to separate the "story" from the question. For example:

7. You have decided to buy 100 shares of ABC Mutual Fund, which prices its shares at 5:00 pm every business day. You turn in your order at 3:00 pm when the shares are priced at $10 NAV, $10.86 POP. The sales load is 7.9%. What will your 100 shares cost?

    A. $1,000
    B. $1,079
    C. $1,086
    D. 100 times the offering price that will be calculated at 5:00 pm.

7. **D**. *A clue to the answer is presented in the first sentence—the fund price at 5:00 pm. Orders for mutual funds are executed based on the next price calculated (forward pricing), so the answer to this question is D. You do not need to calculate anything.*

Take the time to identify what the question is asking. Of course, your ability to do so assumes you have studied sufficiently. There is no method for answering questions if you don't know the material.

Recognize synonymous terms

The securities industry has a tendency to abbreviate terms and use acronyms. Terms may be used interchangeably throughout the test, and you should be able to recognize them.

Industry Term	Synonyms or Acronym
effective date	release date
Self Regulatory Organization	SRO
registered representative (RR) account executive (AE)	agent
fidelity bond	surety bond
filing	notice filing

Eliminate/Short-list Roman numeral choices

Roman numeral questions are common on NASD exams and they require you to distinguish between several likely answers. When you are confronted with Roman numeral choices, try to eliminate one or two of them to help narrow your choices. For example, if you can eliminate choice II in a Roman numeral question, and three of the four answers contain choice II, you have narrowed down your options to the correct answer by process of elimination.

8. An owner of common stock has which of the following rights?

I. Right to determine when dividends will be issued
II. Right to vote at stockholders' meetings or by proxy
III. Right to determine the amount of any dividends issued
IV. Right to buy redeemed shares before they are offered to the public

A. I, III and IV only
B. II only
C. II, III and IV only
D. II and IV only

8. **B**. *Stockholders have the right to vote on certain corporate matters and the right to dividends, if and when declared. Stockholders do not vote on when a dividend is to be paid, nor on the amount of dividend to be paid. Knowing this, you can eliminate answers A and C.*

Beware of changing answers   If you are unsure of an answer, your first hunch is most likely to be correct. **Do not** change answers on the exam without a good reason. In general, change an answer only if you discover that you did not read the question correctly or find new or additional helpful information in another question.

Pace yourself   Some people finish the exam early; others use the entire time, and some cannot finish all the questions. Watch the time carefully (time remaining will be displayed on your computer screen) and pace yourself through the exam. Do not dwell on a question if you simply do not know the answer. Make your best guess, mark the question *Record for Review,* and return if time allows.

Dearborn Class Scheduling

Dearborn offers many exam preparation classes throughout the country. For scheduling information, contact:

Dearborn Customer Service at 1-800-824-8742

Our efficient and friendly Customer Service team will be happy to help you with your exam preparation scheduling. .

And remember to visit **www.dearborn.com** for updated industry information and *free* Test Alerts!

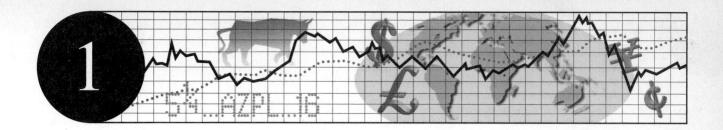

Registration of Persons

INTRODUCTION

The **Uniform Securities Act (USA)** defines the jurisdiction and powers of the state securities Administrator over securities, as well as those persons over which the Administrator (the person in charge of the USA in your state) can apply those powers. For a person to be covered (regulated) by the USA, they must be included in the definition as stated in the law. This unit defines those persons covered by the USA who are subject to the Administrator's jurisdiction and registration requirements.

We will also address the **National Securities Markets Improvements Act of 1996**, usually referred to as **NSMIA**. This federal act separated the responsibility for registration of investment advisers and certain securities between the states and the Securities and Exchange Commission (SEC). Advisers registered with the SEC are called federal covered advisers. Federal covered securities will be discussed in Unit 2.

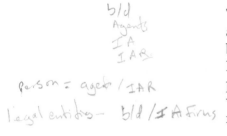

The USA regulates four classes of persons: broker/dealers, agents, investment advisers, and investment adviser representatives. Persons under the USA can be individuals (such as agents and investment adviser representatives) or **legal entities** (such as broker/dealers and investment advisory firms). All persons who fall under the definition of agent or broker/dealer must register with the Administrator. Many investment advisers and investment adviser representatives must register as well.

The Series 63 exam will include approximately 18 questions on the material presented in this unit.

UNIT OBJECTIVES

When you have completed this unit, you should be able to:

- recognize the distinctions between a natural person and a legal person;
- define broker/dealer, agent, investment adviser, and investment adviser representative;
- identify procedures and requirements for registration in a state; and

- describe the differences between exclusions from definitions and exemptions from registration.

Persons Regulated by the Uniform Securities Act

The Uniform Securities Act regulates four classes of **persons**, each of which has a specific meaning within the language of the act. The four classes of persons are: **broker/dealers**, **agents**, **investment advisers**, and **investment adviser representatives**.

 Take Note: The Administrator is the person in charge of enforcing the Uniform Securities Act in the states.

Legal Definition of Person

Know that the concept of **person** in law can have one of the two following meanings:

- a **natural person** (an individual, human being); or
- a **legal person** (entity) such as a corporation or partnership.

A **natural person** means any individual or person (human being) as the term is used in common, non-legal conversation.

A **legal person** or **legal entity** (such as a corporation) is what is called a legal fiction—it exists as a creature of law. For a legal entity (such as a corporation) to be sued in court, it must have a **legal existence** or **identity**. In addition to corporations, entities such as partnerships and governments are given legal identity as persons under the USA. They can conduct business, commit criminal acts, bear civil liabilities, and be sued in a court of law.

 Take Note: The term person is very broad in scope. However, not all persons are required to register with the Administrator. If a person, whether an individual or organization, does not fall within a definition as the term is used in the act, then the individual (human being) or organization (legal person) is not subject to the registration requirements of the USA. For instance, not all individuals selling securities meet the definition of *agent* and many broker/dealers are excluded from the USA's definition. If an individual or business organization falls within a definition, it is subject to the regulations of the act. Under the USA, definitions are critical.

"Person" includes any entity such as:

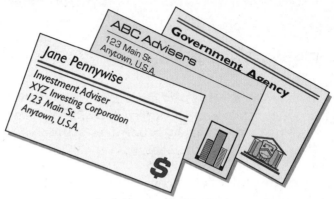

Individual or Business or Government

🖉 **Quick Quiz 1.1**   True or False?

____ 1. A corporation is not a person and therefore the state Administrator does not have jurisdiction over its securities activities.

____ 2. An individual is a natural person and not a legal person subject to the jurisdiction of the Uniform Securities Act.

Answers   *1.* **F.** *A corporation is a person under the law and subject to the jurisdiction of the state Administrator with respect to securities transactions.*

2. **F.** *An individual is a natural person and, just like a legal person (e.g., a corporation), may be subject to the Uniform Securities Act.*

Persons Subject to State Registration

The four classes of persons that fall within the regulatory authority of the Uniform Securities Act are:

- broker/dealers (legal persons, companies);
- agents (natural persons, individuals);
- investment advisers (legal persons, companies); and
- investment adviser representative (natural persons, individuals).

PFA assistant
28,000

Broker/Dealer

A **broker/dealer** is defined as any person (legal entity) engaged in the business of effecting transactions in securities for the accounts of others or for its own account. Any legal person (e.g., a securities firm) with an established place of business (an office) in the state that is in the business of buying and selling securities for the accounts of others (customers) and/or for its own proprietary account is a broker/dealer.

✓ *Take Note:* When a broker/dealer effects trades for the accounts of others, it is acting in an agency capacity—that is, as a broker. When the broker/dealer engages in trades for its own account, it is acting in a principal capacity—that is, as a dealer.

Exclusions from the Definition of Broker/Dealer

In the Uniform Securities Act, the term **broker/dealer** does not include **agents** (because they represent the broker/dealer and therefore are *not* the broker/dealer) and **issuers of securities**.

✓ *Take Note:* The term *exclusion* means "not included in or covered by a definition." The exam focuses more on who is not a broker/dealer than who is one.

Financial institutions are also excluded from the definition because they are covered (regulated) by federal or other legislation. Financial institutions include banks, savings and loan institutions, trust companies, insurance companies, investment companies (as defined by the Investment Company Act of 1940), pension and profit-sharing trusts, and other institutional buyers.

Additionally, a person that has no place of business in the state is not a broker/dealer if that person effects transactions in the state exclusively with or through:

- issuers;
- other broker/dealers;
- financial institutions (as described above); or
- is licensed in the state in which he maintains a place of business and effects securities transactions solely with existing customers who are not residents of the state in which the transaction takes place (sometimes referred to as the **snowbird** rule in reference to the northerners who winter in the warmer climates of the south and southwestern United States).

Case Study: Exclusion from the Definition of Broker/Dealer

Situation: First Securities Corporation is a registered broker/dealer with offices in Illinois. Mr. Thompson, a registered representative in First Securities' Illinois office, recommends the purchase of Simus Shoes stock to his customer, Mr. Bixby, who is temporarily on vacation in Hawaii. Mr. Bixby agrees to the purchase of Simus Shoes, as well as other securities, while in Hawaii.

The Hawaiian state securities Administrator does not issue a cease and desist order against First Securities for unlawfully selling securities as an unregistered broker/dealer in Hawaii.

Analysis: The Hawaiian securities Administrator acted correctly by not issuing a cease and desist order against First Securities. Under the USA, First Securities is not required to register as a broker/dealer in Hawaii because it limits its business to an existing customer, Mr. Bixby, who is temporarily in the state. Since First Securities is properly registered in Illinois, it need not register in Hawaii providing, of course, Mr. Bixby does not take up permanent residence there.

☼ **Test Topic Alert!**   ✓ *Take Note:* When an existing client legally changes residence to another state in which the broker/dealer is not registered, the firm has a 30-day period during which it may continue to do business with that client without registration in the new state. Should it wish to continue to maintain that client, the broker/dealer would have to register in that state.

✓ *Take Note:* A broker/dealer that is registered in Canada that does not have a place of business in this state is permitted to effect transactions in securities with a client from Canada who now lives in this state if those transactions are in a self-directed tax advantaged retirement plan (similar to an IRA), of which the individual client is the holder or contributor in Canada.

Broker/Dealer Registration Requirements

The USA is very clear regarding the registration requirements of broker/dealers. It states: "*It is unlawful for any person to transact business in this state as a broker/dealer...unless he is registered under this Act.*"

If a person falls within the definition of a broker/dealer, that person must register. If a person is excluded from the definition, they do not have to register.

Financial Requirements

The Administrator may establish **minimum capital requirements** for broker/dealers. These requirements may not exceed those provided for under the Securities Exchange Act of 1934. No minimum financial requirements for agents or investment adviser representatives exist; however, the Administrator may require those broker/dealers and investment advisers who have custody of, or discretionary authority over, clients funds or securities to post surety bonds. The amount of surety bonds, sometimes called **fidelity bonds**, is limited to the amount set by the Securities Exchange Act of 1934.

✓ *Take Note:* The Administrator may require that broker/dealers and investment advisers meet certain financial standards. In general, registrants must submit an application with the required information, provide a consent to service of process, and pay filing fees to the state.

Case Study:
Who Is a
Broker/Dealer?

Situation: First Securities Corporation of Illinois sells municipal bonds and equity securities to both the general public and to other securities firms. First Securities sells many of its municipal bonds to its biggest customer, Transitions Broker/Dealers, Inc., located in Indiana. Transition Brokers is a wholesale broker/dealer with no offices in Illinois that trades exclusively with other broker/dealers.

First Securities discovers that Transition Brokers/Dealers is not registered in Illinois but does business with other broker/dealers in Illinois. The president of First Securities asks the president of Transition Brokers why his firm is not registered in Illinois; the president of Transition answers that it is because they are not broker/dealers in Illinois. The president of First Securities is baffled—it appears to him that Transition is indeed a broker/dealer.

Analysis: First Securities sells both exempt securities (municipal bonds) and nonexempt securities (equities) to the general public and to other broker-dealers. First Securities is a broker/dealer because it is a legal entity with a place of business in the state that effects securities transactions for itself and for the accounts of others and so must register in Illinois.

Like First Securities, Transition Broker/Dealer conducts broker/dealer activities. However, in Illinois it confines the business to transactions between itself and other broker/dealers, such as First Securities. The USA specifically excludes from the definition of *broker/dealer* out-of-state broker/dealers who deal exclusively with other broker/dealers and have no place of business in the state.

While Transition Brokers is in **fact** conducting operations of a broker/dealer in Illinois, it does not meet the definition as stated in the USA and, therefore, it is not subject to registration with the Illinois securities Administrator. If Transition Brokers were located or had an office in Illinois, it would be a broker/dealer by definition and have to register as such in Illinois.

What about the Indiana Administrator? Which of the firms must register? Even though Transition Brokers only does a wholesale business, since it has an office in the state of Indiana, it would meet the definition of broker/dealer and would have to register as such. What about First Securities? Well, it depends on several factors we haven't been told. Does First Securities maintain an office in Indiana? If it does, registration is required. If it doesn't and the only securities business it does is with other broker/dealers and financial institutions, then it does not have to register in Indiana.

✏ Quick Quiz 1.2

True or False?

___ 1. In general, a person who effects transactions in securities for itself or for the account of others in the course of business, must register in the state as a broker/dealer.

___ 2. Under the Uniform Securities Act, an out-of-state firm that transacts business with an established customer who is on vacation is not considered a broker in the state in which the customer is on vacation.

___ 3. A person not defined as a broker/dealer in the state under the USA need not register as such.

Answers

1. **T.** A person who effects transactions in securities for itself or for the account of others must register in the state as a broker/dealer unless specifically excluded from the definition.

2. **T.** A firm with an out-of-state registration is not considered a broker/dealer in that state if transacting business with a customer who is passing through the state on vacation.

3. **T.** If a person is excluded from the definition, that person need not register as a broker/dealer; however, if they are not excluded, they must register.

Agent

The Uniform Securities Act defines an **agent** as any individual who represents a broker/dealer (legal entity) or an issuer (legal entity) in effecting (or attempting to effect) transactions in securities.

Agents are individuals in a sales capacity who represent broker/dealers or issuers of securities. As agents, they act on behalf of others who are known as **principals**. Agents are often referred to as **sales representatives** or **registered representatives** whether selling registered or exempt securities.

✓ **Take Note:** The use of the term *individual* here is important. Only an individual, or a natural person, can be an agent. A corporation, such as a brokerage firm, is not a natural person—it is a legal entity. The brokerage firm is the legal person (legal entity) that the agent (natural person) represents in securities transactions.

agent = Natural person

brokerage firm = legal entity (legal person)

Non-Registered Employees of Broker/Dealers

Clerical and administrative employees of a broker/dealer are generally not included in the definition of agent and, therefore, are not required to be registered.

 For Example: Secretaries and sales assistants (known as ministerial personnel) are not agents if their activities are confined to administrative activities. However, if secretaries or sales assistants accept customer transactions or take orders over the phone, they are engaging in securities transactions and are subject to registration as agents.

Exclusions from the Definition of Agent

The USA excludes from the definition of agent those individuals who represent issuers when effecting transactions in the following three situations:

- securities exempt from registration;
- transactions exempt from registration; and
- with existing employees, partners, or directors of an issuer if no commissions or remuneration is given for soliciting in the state.

In all of these instances, the exclusion applies only if no commissions or remuneration, direct or indirect, is given for soliciting in the state.

Effecting Transactions in Exempt Securities

Securities exempt from registration are called **exempt securities.** An employee of an issuer is not an agent when representing an issuer in the following exempt securities:

- US government and municipal securities;
- Canadian government and other securities as specified by the Administrator;
- securities of US banks and savings institutions or trust companies;
- commercial paper rated in the top three categories by the major rating agencies with denominations of $50,000 or more with maturities of nine months or less; and
- investment contracts issued in connection with employee's stock purchase, savings, pensions, or profit-sharing plans.

Once again, the exclusion from the definition of agent only applies when the individual does not receive any type of compensation that is related to the amount or type of sales made.

Effecting Exempt Transactions

Transactions exempt from registration are called **exempt transactions**. They are:

- isolated nonissuer transactions;
- transactions between issuer and underwriters;
- transactions between savings institutions or trust companies; or
- private placements.

Exempt security and exempt transaction will be covered in thorough detail in the next unit.

Effecting Transactions with Existing Employees, Partners, or Directors of an Issuer

An employee of an issuer is not an agent when selling his employer's securities to existing employees, partners, or directors if no direct or indirect compensation is earned. If earnings are in any way tied to sales, the employee would be an agent and have to register as such under the act.

 Take Note: An employee of an issuer is not an agent when representing an issuer if the issue is exempt from registration (e.g., banks, financial institutions, and governments). Additionally, the employee is not an agent when representing an issuer in exempt transactions (transactions between an underwriter and issuer). If the individual receives any type of compensation that is based upon sales, registration as an agent is required.

Agent Registration Requirements

The registration requirements for an agent are similar to those for a broker/dealer. The USA states: *It is unlawful for any person to transact business in this state as...an agent unless he is registered under this act.*

Financial Requirements

In general there are no financial requirements, or **net worth requirements**, to register as an agent, but an agent's registration can be terminated in the case of insolvency. The Administrator may require an agent to be bonded.

Case Study: Agent as Defined by the USA

Situation: The City of Chicago issues bonds for the maintenance of local recreational facilities. Purchasers have two choices: they can purchase the bonds directly from the city through Charles Stith (an employee of the city responsible for selling the bonds) or they can purchase them from Mr. Thompson (an employee of First Securities Corporation of Chicago). Neither Mr. Stith nor Mr. Thompson charge a commission, although First Securities Corp. is remunerated with an underwriting fee.

Analysis: The City of Chicago is an issuer of exempt securities (municipal bonds). Charles Stith, as an employee of the issuer (City of Chicago), is not an agent as defined in the USA because he is representing the issuer in the sale of an exempt security and is receiving no sales-based compensation. Therefore, Stith does not need to register as an agent with the Administrator of Illinois. However, Thompson, as a representative of First Securities, must register with the Administrator because he represents a broker/dealer in effecting securities transactions in the state. Representatives (agents of broker/dealers) must register in the states in which they sell securities.

 Take Note: Exemptions from registration generally apply to representatives of issuers, rather than to representatives of broker/dealers. If Mr. Stith received a bonus based upon sales production, the USA would consider that as commission compensation and Mr. Stith would have to register as an agent.

Fee and Commission Sharing

Registered agents of broker/dealers may share fees or split commissions with others provided they are registered as agents for the same broker/dealer or for a broker/dealer under common ownership or control.

Multiple Registrations An individual may not act at any one time as an agent for more than one broker/dealer or for more than one issuer, unless the broker/dealers or issuers for whom the agent acts are affiliated by direct or indirect common control or the Administrator, by rule or order, authorizes multiple licenses.

✏ **Quick Quiz 1.3**   Write **A** if the person is an agent and **B** if not.

_A_ 1. Person who effects transactions in municipal securities on behalf of a broker/dealer.

_B_ 2. A registered representative's salaried secretary who takes orders.

_A_ 3. An employee of a bank that is issuing shares who receives a commission for selling the bank's securities.

_A_ 4. Individual who represents her nonexempt employer in the sale of its securities to existing employees for a commission.

_B_ 5. Person who represents an issuer in effecting transactions with underwriters.

Answers   1. **A.** Persons must be registered as agents when they effect transactions on behalf of broker/dealers whether the securities are exempt or not.

2. **A.** Secretaries effecting transactions on behalf of a broker/dealer must be registered whether or not they receive a commission.

3. **A.** An employee who represents an issuer of exempt securities (a bank) in selling its securities must register as an agent if they receive commissions. If no compensation were involved, then registration would not be required because such an individual is not an agent.

4. **A.** A person who represents an employer in selling securities to employees must register as an agent if the person receives a commission. If no commission is paid, registration is not necessary.

5. **B.** Persons who represent issuers in securities transactions with underwriters need not register as agents as long as no compensation is paid. In the absence of a statement to the contrary, assume that there is no compensation.

Investment Adviser

Under the USA, an **investment adviser** is defined as any person who, for compensation and as part of a regular business, engages in the business of advising others as to the value of securities or as to the advisability of investing in or selling them. The advice can be delivered in person, through publications or writings, or through research reports concerning securities.

To be an investment adviser, a person must meet the following three requirements. They must:

- provide advice about securities;
- provide that advice as part of an ongoing business; and
- receive compensation for the investment advisory services.

✓ ***Take Note:*** The USA's definition parallels that of the Investment Advisers Act of 1940, the federal law. In 1987, the SEC published release IA-1092 that further expanded the definition to include many financial planners and sports/entertainment agents.

In most cases, investment advisers are legal persons—that is, partnerships or corporations that provide investment advice or portfolio management services on an ongoing basis.

✓ ***Take Note:*** An individual can be an investment adviser if he operates as a **sole proprietorship**.

✓ ***Take Note:*** Advice given on investments not defined as securities, such as rare coins, art, and real estate, is not considered investment advice for purposes of the USA.

Exclusions from Definition of Investment Adviser

There are many exclusions from the term **investment adviser**. Excluded are the following.

- Investment adviser representatives (the firm is the investment adviser)
- Banks, savings institutions, and trust companies
- Lawyers, Accountants, Teachers, and Engineers (LATE) whose investment advisory services are solely incidental to their professional practices
- Broker/dealers whose investment advisory services are incidental to their brokerage business and who receive no special or separate compensation for offering advice
- A publisher, employee, or columnist of a newspaper, news magazine, or business or financial publication; or an owner, operator, producer, or employee of cable, radio, or television network, station, or production facility if, in either case, the financial or business news published or disseminated is made available to the general public and the content does not consist of rendering advice on the basis of the specific investment situation of each client

- • Federal covered investment advisers (advisers with more than $30 million under management)
- • Any other person the Administrator specifies

Registration Requirements for an Investment Adviser

The registration requirements for an investment adviser are much like those of a broker/dealer. The USA states: "It is unlawful for any person to transact business in this state as an investment adviser. . . unless he is so registered under this act or is exempt from registration requirements."

Exemption from Registration for Investment Advisers

The USA specifically exempts from registration certain persons who, although they fall within the definition of an investment adviser, do not have to register as such in the state.

The advisers exempt from registration with the state Administrator are those who have no place of business in the state but are registered in another state, provided their only clients in the state are:

- • broker/dealers registered under the act;
- • investment advisers;
- • institutional investors including large employee benefit plans;
- • existing clients who are not residents but are temporarily in the state;
- • limited to five or fewer clients other than those listed above resident in the state during the preceding 12 months (called the *de minimis* exemption); or
- • any others the Administrator exempts by rule or order.

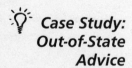

Case Study: Out-of-State Advice

Situation: A California-registered investment adviser, with no offices located in any other state, has directed investment advice on five separate occasions over the past year to individual residents of the state of Nevada. Is the investment adviser required to register in the state of Nevada?

Analysis: The answer is no. Registration is not required because the investment adviser does not have an office in Nevada and directs business to five or fewer individual residents of the state during the year. If the firm had an office in Nevada, registration would be required in that state. Also, even if the firm had no office in Nevada, registration would be required if business had been transacted with six or more individual residents of the state during the previous 12 months. If the business had been transacted with other investment advisers, broker/dealers, or institutional investors, there is no limit as long as there is no office in the state.

✔ **Take Note:** NSMIA eliminated state registration requirements for advisers with $30 million or more in assets under management. Advisers with between $25 to $30 million have the option to register with either the state or the SEC. Advisers with less than $25 million must register with the state. NSMIA also stated that pension consultants with assets under control of at least $50 million would also be federal covered advisers.

✔ **Take Note:** Investment advisers exempt from state registration are *not* exempt from paying state filing fees and giving notice to the Administrator. The procedure followed is called **notice filing.**

Case Study:
Exclusion from
Definition and
Exemptions from
Registration

Situation: Charles & Goode, a partnership located in Illinois, has been in the business of selling investment advice in the form of research reports and managing securities portfolios for the past 20 years. The partnership has earned a good reputation among investors and has managed less than $25 million until this year. This year they gained several new clients and now have $50 million in assets under management.

Most of Charles & Goode's clients are wealthy individuals and residents of Illinois, but they have three clients who are residents of Wisconsin and 30 clients who live in Indiana. The principals of Charles & Goode have also formed a separate partnership called the C&G Mutual Fund Advisers, Inc., which manages a small investment company with assets of $15 million. The partners in Charles & Goode are uncertain about what they must do to be in compliance with the Uniform Securities Act.

Analysis: As a partnership in the business of managing money for individual clients, Charles & Goode falls within the definition of an investment adviser and must so register with the Illinois securities Administrator until it manages $25 million or more in assets. However, with the addition of new clients as of the current year, Charles & Goode will be exempt from registration with Illinois, although it still falls within the definition of an investment adviser. Charles & Goode is now a federal covered adviser that must register with the SEC because it has more than $30 million in assets.

Prior to becoming a federal covered adviser, Charles & Goode need not register in Wisconsin because they have five or fewer clients in the state; however, they would have to register in Indiana because they have more than five clients there. After becoming federal covered advisers, Charles & Goode does not have to register in Indiana, Wisconsin, or Illinois—after it manages more than $30 million it only has to register with the SEC, not the state Administrator. An adviser with assets between $25 and $30 million may register with either the state or the SEC. Advisers with $30 million or more in assets must register with the SEC only.

The separate partnership, C&G Mutual Fund Advisers Inc., which manages only $15 million, is exempt from registration in Illinois (or any other state) because those persons who operate as investment advisers to investment companies registered under the Investment Company Act of 1940, regardless of the size of the investment company, are included in the definition of federal covered adviser.

✓ **Take Note:** As a general rule, the SEC or federal rules involve bigger numbers than the state rules—large investment advisers must register with the SEC; small investment advisers must register with the state.

Adviser managing . . .

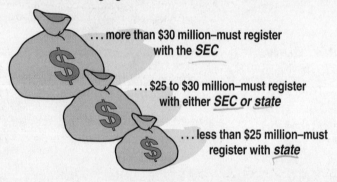

. . . more than $30 million–must register with the **SEC**

. . . $25 to $30 million–must register with either **SEC or state**

. . . less than $25 million–must register with **state**

Financial Requirements

The Administrator may, by rule or order, establish minimal financial requirements for an investment adviser registered in the state. The Administrator may require an adviser who has custody of or discretionary authority over client funds or securities to post bonds or another form of security. The financial requirements that the Administrator sets cannot exceed those required by federal law. Usually, the bond is higher for custody than for discretion. Typically, the bond required of investment advisers with discretionary authority is $10,000 while those maintaining custody of customer funds and/or securities will need a bond or net worth of $35,000.

Like all other persons required to be registered, an investment adviser must pay a filing fee as determined by the Administrator.

✓ **Take Note:** In lieu of the surety bond, the Administrator will generally accept cash or marketable securities.

Quick Quiz 1.4

Choose **A** if the phrase describes an investment adviser that must register under the USA and **B** if it does not.

 1. Publisher of a newspaper that renders general financial advice.

 2. Broker/dealer that charges a fee for providing investment advice over and above commissions from securities transactions.

___ 3. An investment adviser that manages $10 million in assets.

Answers

1. **B.** Publishers of newspapers and magazines of general circulation that offer general financial advice need not register.

2. **A.** Broker/dealers must register as investment advisers if they receive special or separate compensation for giving investment advice.

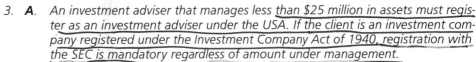

3. **A.** An investment adviser that manages less than $25 million in assets must register as an investment adviser under the USA. If the client is an investment company registered under the Investment Company Act of 1940, registration with the SEC is mandatory regardless of amount under management.

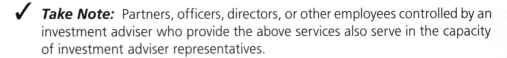

Investment Adviser Representative

An **investment adviser representative** means any individual (other than an investment adviser or federal covered investment adviser) who represents an investment adviser or federal covered investment adviser when:

- making investment recommendations;
- managing accounts or client portfolios;
- soliciting investment advisory services; or
- supervising employees who perform any of these duties.

✓ **Take Note:** Partners, officers, directors, or other employees controlled by an investment adviser who provide the above services also serve in the capacity of investment adviser representatives.

Investment Advisers and Investment Adviser Representatives

Investment Adviser: Business or Individual

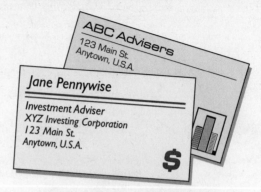

**Investment Adviser Representative:
Individual Only**

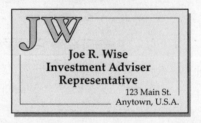

Exclusions from the Definition of Investment Adviser Representative	Employees of investment advisory firms are excluded from the term **investment adviser representative**, provided their activities are confined to clerical duties or those activities which are solely incidental to the investment advisory services offered. Should the investment advisory employee receive specific compensation for offering these services, the employee would then have to register as an investment adviser representative.

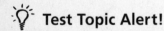 **Test Topic Alert!**

Registration of a broker/dealer leads to automatic agent registration of partners, officers, or directors active in the business and anyone else performing a similar function. Registration of an investment adviser leads to automatic investment adviser representative registration of the same category of persons. Examinations may be required.

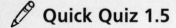 **Quick Quiz 1.5**

True or False?

____ 1. An investment adviser representative must register with the SEC if she has clients with assets of $30 million or more under management.

____ 2. An investment adviser maintaining custody of a customer's securities and/or funds and exercising discretion in the account is generally required to maintain a minimum net worth of $35,000.

____ 3. An employee of an investment advisory firm is an investment adviser representative if his duties are confined to clerical activities.

_F_ 4. An administrative employee who receives specific compensation for offering investment advisory services is not an investment adviser representative.

_T_ 5. An employee of an investment advisory firm is an investment adviser representative if his duties involve making investment recommendations.

Answers

1. **F.** An investment adviser (not the investment representative) must register with the SEC if the firm manages assets of $30 million or more. The individual would have to be registered as an investment adviser representative in the state in which her office is located.

2. **F.** The usual net worth requirement for an investment adviser exercising discretion is $10,000 while that for one maintaining custody is $35,000. If the adviser does both, only the higher number applies.

3. **F.** An employee of an investment advisory firm is not an investment adviser representative if his duties are confined to clerical activities.

4. **F.** An administrative employee who receives specific compensation for offering investment advisory services is considered an investment adviser representative.

5. **T.** An employee of an investment advisory firm is an investment adviser representative if his duties involve making investment recommendations.

General Registration Procedures

Any person who meets the definition of broker/dealer, agent, investment adviser, or investment adviser representative must register with the state. To register with the state securities Administrator, a person must:

- submit an application;
- provide a consent to service of process;
- pay filing fees;
- post a bond (if required by the Administrator); and
- take and pass an examination if required by the Administrator. The examination may be written, oral, or both.

Submit Application All persons must complete and submit an **initial application** (as well as renewals) to the state securities Administrator. The application must contain whatever information the Administrator may require by rule, and may include the following.

- Form and place of business (broker/dealers and investment advisers)
- Proposed method of doing business

- Qualifications and business history (broker/dealers and investment advisers must include the qualifications and history of partners, officers, directors, and other persons with controlling influence over the organization)
- Injunctions and administrative orders
- Convictions of misdemeanors involving a security or any aspect of the securities business
- Felony convictions, whether securities related or not
- Financial condition and history
- Advertising and promotional material, if applicant is an investment adviser
- Form ADV or similar document if an investment adviser

In the case of an investment adviser, the Administrator also may require that an applicant publish an announcement of the registration in one or more newspapers in the state.

 Take Note: If an agent terminates employment with a broker/dealer, both parties must promptly notify the Administrator.

If an agent terminates employment with Broker/Dealer I to join Broker/Dealer II, all three parties must notify the Administrator. If an investment adviser representative terminates employment with an investment adviser, it depends upon how the investment adviser is registered.

If it is a state registered adviser, then the firm must notify the Administrator. If it is a federal covered adviser, then the investment adviser representative must be the one to notify the Administrator.

Provide Consent to Service of Process

New applicants for registration must provide the Administrator of every state in which they intend to register with a **consent to service of process**. The consent to service of process appoints the Administrator as the applicant's attorney to receive and process non-criminal securities-related complaints against the applicant. Under the consent to service of process, all complaints received by the Administrator have the same legal effect as if they had been served personally on the applicant.

 Take Note: The consent to service of process is submitted with the initial application and remains in force permanently. It does not need to be supplied with each renewal of a registration.

Pay Initial and Renewal Filing Fees

States require **filing fees** for initial applications as well as for renewal applications. If an application is withdrawn or denied, the Administrator is entitled to retain a portion of the fee. Filing fees for broker/dealers, investment advisers, and their representatives need not be identical. Broker/dealers and investment advisers may file, without a fee, for a successor firm to complete the unexpired portion of the year. The renewal date for all registrations is December 31.

Financial Reports and Recordkeeping Requirements

The USA requires registered broker/dealers and investment advisers to keep such accounts, correspondence, memoranda, papers, books, and other records as the Administrator requires. These records must be preserved for three years by broker/dealers and five years by advisers unless the Administrator prescribes otherwise. All records must be readily accessible (in the office) for the first two years.

The Administrator may also require registered broker/dealers and investment advisers to file financial reports. The recordkeeping and financial reports required by the state Administrator may not exceed those required by the Securities Exchange Act of 1934 or the Investment Advisers Act of 1940.

If any material information in these documents becomes inaccurate or incomplete, the registrant must promptly file a corrected copy with the Administrator. All required documents are subject to reasonable periodic, special, or other examination as the Administrator deems appropriate, in the public interest, or for the protection of the investor.

✓ **Take Note:** The Administrator's authority does not stop at the state line. The administrator of any state that the registrant is registered in may demand an inspection during reasonable business hours with whatever frequency the Administrator deems necessary.

Post Bonds

The Administrator may, by rule, require **minimum net capital** for broker/dealers. Broker/dealers in compliance with the SEC net capital requirement are exempt from the USA's minimum capital requirements. Agents of broker/dealers do not have net worth requirements; however, the Administrator may require an agent to post a surety bond if the agent has discretion over client funds or securities.

Effectiveness of Registration

Unless a legal proceeding is instituted or the applicant is notified that the application is incomplete, the license of a broker/dealer, agent, investment adviser or investment adviser representative becomes effective at noon, 30 days after the later of the date an application for licensing is filed and is complete or the date an amendment to an application is filed and is complete. An application is complete when the applicant has furnished information responsive to each applicable item of the application. The Administrator by order may authorize an earlier effective date of licensing.

Quick Quiz 1.6

True or False?

_F_ 1. A consent to service of process must be submitted with each renewal application.

___ 2. An Administrator may establish net capital requirements for investment adviser representatives.

_F_ 3. When a securities professional registers in a state, he must provide the state Administrator with a list of all states he intends to register in.

Answers

1. **F.** A consent to service of process is filed with the initial application and permanently remains on file with the Administrator.

2. **F.** The term net capital requirement *refers to the financial requirements of a broker/dealer, not an investment adviser representative. Investment adviser representatives may be required to post a bond if they maintain discretion or custody of client funds and/or securities.*

3. **F.** A list of other states in which a securities professional intends to register is not required on a state application for registration.

Registration of Persons HotSheet

Person:
- Individual, company, association, or government

Broker/Dealer Registration:
- Must register in state where business is done unless exempt
- Effective after Administrator notification; expires December 31

Exempt from State Registration as a Broker/Dealer:
- Banks, savings institutions, other financial institutions, agents, issuers
- Broker/dealers with no office in state only doing business with institutions
- Broker/dealers registered in another state transacting business with a current client passing through a different state

Exemptions from Agent Registration:
- Represents issuer in exempt transaction
- Represents issuer in exempt securities
- Represents issuer in sale of employee benefits plans
- Must not receive compensation that is sale related

Agent Registration:
- Agents must be registered in state of residence of the client where securities are offered, and where securities are sold

- Agents who represent broker/dealers must be registered if they sell exempt or nonexempt securities
- Broker/dealers can only employ registered agents
- Agents who represent issuers generally must be registered if they sell nonexempt securities
- Effective after Administrator notification, no later than noon of the 30th day; expires December 31
- Notification by agent & old & new broker/dealer for employment change
- Notification by state registered investment adviser or investment adviser representative of federal covered adviser for employment change
- Automatic registration of partners, officers, and directors when new broker/dealers and investment advisers register

Investment Adviser Registration:

- Federally registered if adviser manages more than $30 million
- State registered if adviser manages less than $25 million
- Choice between federal and state if adviser manages between $25 and $30 million
- Investment company advisers are always federally registered
- File form ADV and appropriate fees
- Effective after Administrator notification, no later than noon of the 30th day; expires December 31

Investment Adviser Exemptions:

- No office in state and communications directed to 5 or fewer individual residents of the state in 12 months
- No office in state and clients are institutions, broker/dealers, or investment advisers only

Investment Adviser Recordkeeping:

- All specific customer and investment adviser records kept for 5 years; must be kept in investment adviser's office for the first 2 years

Broker/Dealer Recordkeeping:

- Same as investment adviser except 3 years instead of 5 years

كتاب ®

١٢٠ كـ
١٥٠ ٨٠٪

Series 63
Unit Test 1

1. Which of the following would be an agent under the terms of the USA?

   I. A sales representative of a licensed bro-ker/dealer who sells secondary securities to the general public
   II. An assistant to the president of a bro-ker/dealer who, for administrative purposes, accepts orders on behalf of the senior partners
   III. A subsidiary of a major commercial bank registered as a broker/dealer that sells securities to the public
   IV. An issuer of nonexempt securities registered in the state and sold to the general public

   A. I and II only
   B. III and IV only
   C. I, II and III only
   D. I, II, III and IV

2. A publicly traded corporation offers its employees an opportunity to purchase shares of the company's common stock directly from the issuer. A specific employee of the company is designated to process any orders for that stock. Under the USA, the employee

   A. must register as an agent of the issuer
   B. need not register as an agent of the issuer under any circumstances
   C. may receive commissions without registration
   D. must register as an agent if he will receive commissions or remuneration, either directly or indirectly

3. Registration as an investment adviser under the USA would be required for any firm in the business of giving advice on the purchase of

   A. convertible bonds
   B. gold coins
   C. rare convertible automobiles
   D. apartments undergoing a conversion to condominiums

4. Under the Uniform Securities Act, which of the following qualifies as an investment adviser representative?

   A. An employee, highly skilled in evaluating securities, who performs administrative or clerical functions for an investment adviser
   B. An individual who renders fee-based advice on precious metals
   C. A solicitor for an investment advisory firm who is paid a fee for his services
   D. An agent who offers incidental advice on securities as part of his sales commissions

5. Under the Uniform Securities Act, all of the following persons may provide investment advice incidental to their normal business without requiring registration as an investment adviser EXCEPT a(n)

   A. teacher
   B. economist
   C. lawyer
   D. engineer

6. Which of the following persons is defined as an agent by the Uniform Securities Act?

   A. Silent partner of a broker/dealer
   B. Secretary of a branch office sales manager
   C. Clerk at a broker/dealer who is authorized to take orders
   D. Broker/dealer executive who does not solicit or transact business

7. Under the Uniform Securities Act, any partner, officer, or director of a registered investment adviser is an investment adviser representative if he

   I. offers advice concerning securities
   II. manages client accounts or portfolios
   III. determines securities recommendations for representatives to disseminate
   IV. supervises personnel engaged in the above activities but does not sell these services to the public

   A. I only
   B. I and II only
   C. I, II and III only
   D. I, II, III and IV

8. Under the Uniform Securities Act, an agent is a(n)

   A. broker/dealer who sells registered securities to the general public
   B. individual who represents an issuer in a transaction exempt from the act
   C. individual representing a broker/dealer who sells federal covered securities exempt from registration under the act
   D. individual who represents an issuer in an exempt transaction in which no commissions are paid

9. According to the Uniform Securities Act, which of the following is(are) considered a broker/dealer?

   I. An agent who issues securities for his own account and for clients of his employer
   II. An issuer of securities that are traded on SEC-registered exchanges
   III. A corporation that specializes in the sale of various oil and gas limited partnerships
   IV. A credit union that issues its own stock to depositors in proportion to the amount of the funds on deposit

   A. I only
   B. II only
   C. I and II only
   D. III only

10. Under SEC Release IA-1092, an investment adviser is all of the following EXCEPT a

   I. broker/dealer who charges for investment advice
   II. publisher of a financial newspaper
   III. person who sells security analysis
   IV. CPA who, as an incidental part of his practice, charges a fee for constructing a portfolio of tax-sheltered investments

   A. I and II
   B. II and III
   C. II and IV
   D. III and IV

11. Under the Uniform Security Act, the term person would include all of the following EXCEPT

   I. an unincorporated association
   II. a child prodigy, gifted in math, in the custody of his parents, for whom his parents opened an account at a major securities firm
   III. a political subdivision
   IV. an individual

   A. I, II and IV
   B. III and IV
   C. II and III
   D. II only

12. Under the USA, which of the following is considered a broker/dealer in a state?

   A. First Federal Company Trust
   B. XYZ broker/dealer with an office in the state whose only clients are insurance companies
   C. An agent effecting transactions for a broker/dealer
   D. A broker/dealer with no place of business in the state who only does business with other broker/dealers

13. Who of the following must register as an agent?

   A. An individual representing a broker/dealer who sells commercial paper
   B. An individual who sells commercial paper for ABC National Bank
   C. An employee of the Fed whose job is selling Treasury bonds to the public.
   D. An individual who is paid a commission to sell certificates of deposit for ABC National Bank

14. An Administrator can deny an investment adviser's registration for all of the following reasons EXCEPT

   A. lack of experience
   B. failure to post a surety bond
   C. failure to pass a written exam
   D. not meeting minimum financial standards
   E.

15. Which of the following would meet the definition of investment adviser under the Uniform Securities Act?

   I. A broker/dealer making a separate charge for investment advice
   II. The publisher of a weekly magazine, sold on newsstands, that contains at least 5 stock recommendations per issue
   III. A civil damages attorney who advertises that he is available to assist clients in suggesting appropriate investments for their successful claims
   IV. A finance teacher at a local community college who offers weekend seminars on comprehensive financial planning at a very reasonable price

   A. I only
   B. I, II and III only
   C. I, III, and IV only
   D. I, II, III and IV

Series 63
Unit Test 1
Answers & Rationale

1.   A.   Under the USA, only individuals can be agents. A person who sells securities for a broker/dealer is an agent. An administrative person, such as the assistant to the president of a broker/dealer, is considered an agent if he takes securities orders from the public. Corporate entities are excluded from the definition of an agent. Choice III is a broker/dealer and Choice IV is an issuer.

2.   D.   Under the USA, an individual is an agent when effecting transactions with an issuer's existing employees if commissions are paid. Therefore, choice B cannot be correct as there are cases where the employee would have to register as an agent.

3.   A.   Only those in the business of giving advice on securities are required to register as investment advisers. Only the convertible bonds are securities.

4.   C.   A solicitor is considered an investment adviser representative under the Uniform Securities Act. An employee who performs clerical or administrative functions only is not an investment adviser representative. Precious metals are not securities and, therefore, a person advising on them is not considered an investment representative. An agent is a representative of a broker/dealer and as long as the only form of compensation is sales commissions, registration as an investment adviser representative is not required.

5.   B.   The Uniform Securities Act does not grant an economist exemption from registration. The USA does offer an exemption to teachers, lawyers, and engineers if the investment advice is incidental to their business. Remember the acronym LATE—Lawyers, Accountants, Teachers, and Engineers. Do not be fooled by the "e" in "economist."

6.   C.   Anyone who solicits or receives an order while representing a broker/dealer is an agent. Silent partners, administrative personnel, and executives of broker/dealers are not agents under the terms of the USA because they do not solicit or receive orders. Remember, broker/dealers are not agents; agents represent broker/dealers. If, however, any of these individuals were authorized to accept orders, registration as an agent would be required.

7.   D.   The Uniform Securities Act defines persons associated with an investment adviser as an investment adviser representative, including any partner, officer, or director who offers advice concerning securities. Persons who manage client accounts or portfolios, determine securities recommendations, or supervise personnel engaged in the above activities are investment adviser representatives.

8.   C.   An individual employed by a broker/dealer who sells securities to the public is an agent under the Uniform Securities Act. The USA defines "agent" as ". . .any individual other than a broker/dealer who represents a broker/dealer or issuer in effecting or attempting to effect purchases or sales of securities." The law excludes those individuals from the definition of "agent" who represent an issuer in exempt transactions, exempt securities, and transactions with issuers' employees when no commission is paid. There is virtually no case in which a salesperson representing a broker/dealer is not an agent.

9.   D.   A corporation that sells securities to the public, in this case oil and natural gas partnerships, is a broker/dealer as defined by the USA. Agents and securities issuers are not included in the definition of broker/dealer. Credit unions are not considered broker/dealers under the USA.

10. C. A publisher of a financial newspaper and a CPA who, as an incidental part of his practice, constructs portfolios of tax-sheltered investments are not investment advisers. This answer would be the same under both the USA and federal law.

11. D. The term *person* is extremely broad. Excluded from the term would be a minor, a deceased individual, and one who has legally been determined incompetent.

12. B. Any broker/dealer with an office in the state, regardless of the nature of its clients, is defined as a broker/dealer under the USA. If the firm did not have an office in the state and its only clients were institutions such as insurance companies, or other broker/dealers as in Choice D, it would be excluded from the definition. Banks or trust companies (Choice A) and agents (Choice C), are never broker/dealers.

13. A. An individual who represents a broker/dealer who sells commercial paper must register under the USA. The securities (commercial paper) are exempt, nevertheless the representative must be registered as an agent of the broker/dealer. An individual who sells commercial paper for ABC

National Bank would not have to register because the bank is excluded from the definition of broker/dealer and both the transaction and security are exempt from state registration requirements. An employee of the federal government need not register with the state because he represents an exempt issuer and is selling exempt securities without receiving compensation tied to sales. An individual who is paid a commission to sell certificates of deposit for a commercial bank does not have to register as an agent because he is not selling a security.

14. A. Lack of experience, by itself, is not cause for registration denial.

15. C. Publishers of general circulation newspapers and magazines are excluded from the definition of investment adviser, even if the entire publication is devoted to investment advice. A broker/dealer loses its exclusion the moment it offers advice for a separate charge, as does an attorney who holds himself out as offering investment advice. Normally, a teacher is excluded, but not when charging for advice as would appear to be the case here. On this examination, the term "comprehensive financial planning" always includes securities advice.

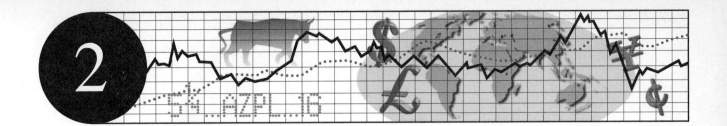

Securities

INTRODUCTION

Just as the Administrator's jurisdiction extends over persons engaged in securities transactions, it also covers the registration of those transactions and securities in the Administrator's state. This unit discusses the procedures for the registration of securities and their exemptions from registration. For a securities transaction to be lawful under the USA, the security itself must be registered unless it is exempt from the act's registration requirements.

The Series 63 exam will include approximately 15 questions on the material presented in this unit.

UNIT OBJECTIVES

When you have completed this unit, you should be able to:

- determine who is and is not a security issuer;
- compare and contrast the different methods of securities registration;
- identify instruments that are securities;
- list the categories of exempt securities;
- define an exempt transaction and provide examples; and
- describe the requirements for exemption from registration for private placements.

Terminology

Recognizing and comprehending terms as they are used in the USA is crucial to understanding the scope and meaning of the act.

Security   Perhaps the most important term in the USA is the term **security**. The provisions of the USA apply to only those financial instruments that are included in the term security. Any instrument that is excluded from the term security is not covered by the act.

While the USA does not explicitly define a security, it provides a comprehensive list of those financial instruments that are included in the term security and are therefore covered by the provisions of the act. Under the USA, **securities** includes:

- note;
- stock;
- treasury stock;
- security future;
- bond;
- debenture;
- evidence of indebtedness;
- certificate of interest or participation in a profit-sharing agreement;
- collateral trust certificate;
- pre-organization certificate or subscription;
- transferable share;
- investment contract;
- voting trust certificate;
- certificate of deposit for a security;
- fractional undivided interest in oil, gas, or other mineral rights;
- put, call, straddle, option, or privilege on a security;
- certificate of deposit, or group or index of securities;
- put, call, straddle, option, or privilege entered into on a national securities exchange relating to foreign currency;
- any interest or instrument commonly known as a security; or
- a certificate of interest or participation in, receipt of, guarantee of, or warrant or right to subscribe to or purchase, any of the above.

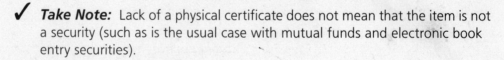 ***Take Note:*** Lack of a physical certificate does not mean that the item is not a security (such as is the usual case with mutual funds and electronic book entry securities).

Not included in the term *security* are:

- an insurance or endowment policy or annuity contract under which an insurance company promises to pay a fixed sum of money either in a lump sum or periodically; and
- interest in a retirement plan such as an IRA or Keogh.

There are four other items that, while attractive investments, the USA does not consider to be included in the definition of security. Those four are:

- collectibles;
- commodities such as precious metals and grains;
- condominiums used as a personal residence; and
- currency.

An antique automobile is a collectible and is not included in the list of terms included in the definition of a security. If a registered agent commits fraud in the sale of this car, he has not committed a violation of the USA. He has violated the antifraud provisions of another act prohibiting fraudulent commercial transactions.

 **Test Topic Alert!**

Have you noticed that there are 20 bulleted items in our listing of security and only six exclusions? The exam will want you to know what *is* and what *is not* a security and we suggest concentrating on learning the six that are NOT, as they are much easier to remember and you will still be able to answer the questions correctly.

✓ **For Example:** Interests in farm animals represent an investment of money in a common effort of others (a breeder or trainer) to realize a profit from the sale of the animals. An individual farmer's direct ownership of a cow is not a security—it is just ownership of a cow. However, a farmer's investment of money in a tradable interest in a herd of cattle, on which he expects to earn a profit solely as the result of the breeder's efforts, is a security because it is an investment contract.

In the same manner, if a condominium is purchased in a resort area with the goal of renting it out most of the year, and it is used only for personal vacation time, the condo would be considered a security as there is a profit motive, typically reliant on the efforts of a third party—the rental agent. On the other hand, if you have chosen to live in a condominium as a personal residence, that's a home, not a security.

Some More Examples

Commodity futures are not securities, but options on commodities are.

Single security futures are securities since they are actually based upon securities.

Annuities with fixed payouts are not securities, but variable annuities are because they are dependent upon the investment performance of securities within the annuity.

 Take Note: The act specifically notes that the term **investment contract** includes interests in a limited partnership, a limited liability company, a limited liability partnership, or an investment in a viatical settlement or similar agreement. The United States Supreme Court, in the **Howey Decision,** determined that an investment contract constitutes an investment in a common enterprise with the expectation of profits to be derived primarily from the efforts of a person other than the investor. A **common enterprise** means an enterprise in which the fortunes of the investor are interwoven with those of either the person offering the investment, a third party, or other investors. Any instrument that is an investment contract is included in the term security.

Nonexempt Security

If a security is not exempt from registration requirements, it is called a **nonexempt security.** When you see the term **nonexempt**, it means *subject to registration*. When you see the term **exempt**, it means *not subject to registration*.

 Take Note: The methods of registration discussed in this unit refer to nonexempt securities because if a security is not exempt from registration, it must be registered.

Issuer

An **issuer** is any person who issues (distributes) or proposes to issue a security. The most common issuers of securities are companies or governments (federal, state, and municipal governments and their agencies and their subdivisions).

 For Example: Simus Shoe Co., (a retail chain store) issues shares to the public. Mr. Bixby (an investor) buys the shares through his broker, Mr. Thompson, at First Securities Corp. Simus Shoe is the issuer; Mr. Bixby is the investor; First Securities Corp. is the broker/dealer; and Mr. Thompson is the registered representative, known in the USA as the agent.

Issuer Transaction

In an issuer transaction, the proceeds of the sale go to the issuer. All new issues are issuer transactions. Some secondary issues, such as the resale of treasury stock, are issuer transactions because the proceeds of the sale go to the issuer, not a third party.

Nonissuer Transaction

A **nonissuer transaction** is not directly, or indirectly, for the benefit of the issuer. A nonissuer transaction occurs when the proceeds from the sale of securities go to the seller of the securities, whether that is an individual or any other selling entity that is not the issuer of those shares. The most common instance of this is everyday trading on the exchanges and Nasdaq.

 Take Note: If Mr. Bixby sells 100 shares of stock he owns in Simus Shoe Co. on the New York Stock Exchange (NYSE), Mr. Bixby receives the proceeds from the sale, not Simus Shoes. This is a nonissuer transaction.

Nonissuer transactions are also referred to as **secondary transactions** or transactions between investors.

✓ **For Example:** When Mr. Bixby sold his 100 shares of Simus Shoe on the NYSE, he sold those shares to another investor who purchased them from him on the floor of the NYSE. This is a secondary transaction.

Initial or Primary Offering

The first time an issuer distributes securities to the public, it is called a **primary** or **initial public offering (IPO)**. Initial or primary offerings are issuer transactions because the issuer (the company) receives the proceeds.

✓ **For Example:** The first time that Simus Shoe Co. issued shares to the public, Simus Shoe engaged in an IPO or a primary offering because it received the proceeds from distributing its shares to the public. After Simus Shoe went public, transactions between investors executed on exchanges through brokerage agents were secondary transactions in nonissuer securities.

Quick Quiz 2.1

1. Which list of instruments below are NOT securities?

   A. Stock, treasury stock, rights, warrants, transferable shares
   B. Voting trust certificates, interests in oil and gas drilling programs
   C. Commodity futures contracts, fixed payment life insurance contracts
   D. Commodity options contracts, interests in multilevel distributorship arrangements

2. The US Supreme Court defined an investment contract as having four components. Which of the following is not part of the four-part test for an investment contract?

   A. An investment of money
   B. An expectation of profit
   C. Management activity by owner
   D. Solely from the efforts of others

3. Nonexempt securities

   A. need not be registered in the state in which they are sold
   B. must always be registered in the state in which they are sold
   C. need not be registered if sold in an exempt transaction
   D. need not be registered if sold in a nonexempt transaction

4. A nonissuer transaction is a transaction

   A. between two corporations where one is issuing the stock and the other is purchasing
   B. in which the issuing corporation will not receive the proceeds from the transaction
   C. where a mutual fund purchases a Treasury Bond directly from the government
   D. in which the security must be registered

Answers

1. **C.** *Commodity futures contracts and fixed payment life insurance contracts are included in our list of 6 items that are not securities. Commodity option contracts are securities.*

2. **C.** *Management activity on the part of the owner is not part of the Howey, or four-part, test for an instrument to be a security. The four parts are: (1) an investment of money in (2) a common enterprise with (3) an expectation of profit (4) solely from the effort of others.*

3. **C.** *Nonexempt securities usually are required to be registered, but not always. If the nonexempt security is sold in an exempt transaction, registration may not be required.*

4. **B.** *A nonissuer transaction is one where the company that issues the shares does not receive the proceeds from the transaction. A nonissuer transaction is a transaction between two investors and may or may not require the security to be registered. Whenever the proceeds go to the issuer, it is an issuer transaction.*

General Procedures for the Registration of Securities

Under the Uniform Securities Act, it is unlawful for any person to offer or sell a security in a state unless the security, transaction, or offer is exempt from the USA's registration requirements. If the security is not exempt or is not a federal covered security, it must be registered in the state or it cannot be lawfully sold in the state.

Registration Procedures

The first step in the registration procedure is for the issuer or its representative to pick up a registration statement or application from the state securities Administrator. The person registering the securities is known as the **registrant**.

Test Topic Alert!   Although most registration statements are filed by the issuer, the exam may require you to know that they may also be filed by any selling stockholder, such as a large block sale by an insider, or a broker/dealer.

Filing the Registration Statement   State Administrators require every issuer to supply the following information on their applications:

- amount of securities to be issued in the state;
- states in which the security is to be offered; and
- any adverse order or judgment concerning the offering by regulatory authorities, court, or the SEC.

When filing the registration statement with the Administrator, an applicant may include documents that have been filed with the Administrator within the last five years, provided the information is current and accurate. The Administrator may, by rule or order, permit the omission of any information it considers unnecessary.

Filing Fee   The issuer (or any other person on whose behalf the offering is to be made) must pay a filing fee as determined by the Administrator when filing the registration. The filing fees are often based upon a percentage of the total offering price.

✓ **Take Note:** If the registration is withdrawn or if the Administrator issues a stop order before the registration is effective, the Administrator may retain a portion of the fee and refund the remainder to the applicant.

Ongoing Reports   The Administrator may require the person who filed the registration statement to file reports to keep the information contained in the registration statement current and to inform the Administrator of the progress of the offering.

✓ **Take Note:** These reports cannot be required more often than quarterly.

Escrow   As a condition of registration, the Administrator may require that a security be placed in **escrow** if the security is issued:

- within the past three years;
- at a price substantially different than the offering price; or
- to any person for a consideration other than cash.

Special Subscription Form

The Administrator may also require, as a condition of registration, that the issue be sold only on a form specified by the Administrator and that a copy of the form or subscription contract be filed with the Administrator or preserved for up to three years.

Effective Registration Period

A registration is effective for one year after its **effective date** (the date that the Administrator authorizes the issuer to sell the shares). However, there is an exception to this rule—the one-year period may be extended if the issuer or broker/dealer offering the securities has an unsold allotment of shares.

✓ **Take Note:** Unlike securities registered under federal law, securities registered under the USA must be reregistered every year.

Withdrawal of Registration Statement

A registration statement may not be withdrawn until one year after its effective date if any securities of the same class are outstanding and may only be withdrawn with the approval of the Administrator.

The Administrator has the power under the USA to deny, suspend, or revoke the registration of a security; however, the Administrator can only invoke these powers if it is in the public's interest and the applicant:

- files a false or incomplete statement;
- is in violation of the USA;
- is engaged in a method of business that is illegal;
- has prepared a fraudulent registration; or
- the underwriter charges unreasonable fees.

In addition, the Administrator may deny a registration if the applicant fails to pay the filing fee. When the fee is paid, the denial order will be removed provided the applicant is in compliance with all registration procedures.

✎ Quick Quiz 2.2

1. With regard to the registration requirements of the Uniform Securities Act, which of the following are TRUE?

    I. Only the issuer itself can file a registration statement with the Administrator.
    II. An application for registration must indicate the amount of securities to be issued in the state.
    III. The Administrator may require registrants to file quarterly reports.

    A. I and II only
    B. I and III only
    C. II and III only
    D. I, II and III

Answers

1. **C.** *The USA requires that any application for registration include the amount of securities to be sold in that state. The Administrator has the power to request regular filings of reports, but no more frequently than quarterly. While the issuer is most commonly the registrant, selling stockholders and broker/dealers may also make application.*

Methods of State Securities Registration

National Securities Markets Improvement Act Of 1996 (NSMIA)

The United States Congress, through its passage of NSMIA, established the SEC as the regulator of nationally based securities activities leaving the states with authority over state-based securities activities.

To clarify the boundaries between federal and state authority, NSMIA established the concept of **covered securities.** Securities covered by federal securities law are exempt from state registration requirements. Therefore, if a security qualifies as a covered security, under federal law, it enjoys a federally imposed exemption from state registration.

Categories of Federal Covered Securities

The major categories of federal covered securities include the following:

- Nationally traded securities—and those specific securities equal to or senior to them
  - Securities listed or authorized for listing on the NYSE and other SEC registered exchanges
  - Securities included or qualified for inclusion in the Nasdaq National Market
- Securities of an investment company registered under the Investment Company Act of 1940
  - Open-end mutual funds
  - Closed-end mutual funds
  - Unit investment trusts
  - Face amount certificates
- Offers and sales of certain exempt securities
  - Securities offered to qualified purchasers under Regulation D of the Securities Act of 1933
  - Securities offered by a municipal/governmental issuer unless the issuer is located in the state in which the securities are being offered
  - Securities offered by an issuer only to its existing security holders if no commission is paid

Notwithstanding the preemptive provisions of NSMIA, state securities Administrators may require certain issuers whose securities are not traded on SEC-registered exchanges or the Nasdaq National Market to file copies of those documents filed with the SEC for notice purposes.

These nonexempt securities issuers must have their securities registered in the states where they intend to sell their securities by following procedures for:

- notice filing;
- coordination; or
- qualification.

Notice Filing   The **notice filing** method of registering an issue—also called **registration by notification** or **registration by filing** applies to issuers who have registered their securities with the SEC under the Securities Act of 1933 but are not exempt from registration with the states in which they intend to distribute their shares. Notice filings are required by securities that are not listed on SEC registered exchanges (e.g., NYSE) or the Nasdaq National Market. Such securities are nonlisted securities that trade interstate as opposed to within one state (intrastate).

State registration under this method is accomplished by filing with the state copies of all records filed with the SEC (including amendments). Securities filing under this method, while they are federally registered, are not federal covered securities exempt from registration in the states in which they are sold.

✓ **Take Note:** States can require the registration of the securities of public offerings by non-bank, non-government issuers whose issues are traded in uncovered marketplaces such as the Nasdaq SmallCap market or the OTC Bulletin Board. States cannot require notice filings from those issues traded on covered exchanges such as the New York Stock Exchange, American Stock Exchange, or the Nasdaq National Market, or any other exchange registered with the SEC.

Qualifications for Notice Filing

To qualify for registration by filing, the issuer must have filed a registration statement with the SEC and accomplished the following.

- Be organized under the laws of the United States or a state or have a designated American agent
- Have been in continuous operation for at least three years and have filed all required reports with the SEC during that time
- Have a class of equity securities of at least 400,000 shares held by at least 500 public shareholders—excluding securities held by officers and directors of the issuer, underwriters, and control persons owning 10% or more of that class of securities (warrants and options held by those persons cannot total more than 10% of the total number of shares)
- Have either:
    - total net worth of $4,000,000, or
    - total net worth of $2,000,000 and net pretax income from operations for two of the last three years
- Not have defaulted in the payment of principal, interest, or dividends in the current fiscal year
- For 30 days the preceding three months, have at least four registered market makers
- Each underwriter of the security must be an NASD member who has agreed to a maximum commission of 10% of the offering price (offering price must be at least $5 per share)

Required Documentation for Notice Filing

To register a security in a state by **notice filing**, consent to service o_
and the following documentation are required:

- a statement demonstrating eligibility for registration by filing;
- the name, address, form of organization of the issuer, the amount of securities to be offered in the state, the states in which the offering will be registered, any adverse judgments pending and a description of the security;
- if part of the offering is made on behalf of a non-issuer, the name, address, amount of securities held by that non-issuer and the reasons for making the offering; and
- a copy of the latest prospectus filed with the registration statement.

If no stop order is in effect or proceeding pending, the documentation has been on file with the Administrator for five days and the filing fee was paid prior to the effectiveness of the federal registration statement, the registration becomes effective concurrently with the federal registration.

If the federal registration statement becomes effective before conditions are met on the state level, the registration statement becomes effective when the conditions are satisfied.

Notice Filing for Federal Covered Investment Companies

Under the USA as amended by NSMIA, the states are prohibited from requiring filings by federal covered issuers. An exemption to this prohibition was made for investment companies. Although investment company securities are federal covered securities, states are permitted to require them to provide notice filings to the states. This exemption was made to allow state securities administrative departments to collect fees in order to offset the costs of the prosecution of fraudulent securities practices in their states.

Under the notice filing procedure, state Administrators may require the issuer to file the following documents as a condition for sale of their securities in the state:

- documents filed with their registration statements filed with the SEC;
- documents filed as amendments to the initial federal registration statement;
- a report as to the value of such securities offered in the state; and
- consent to service of process.

 **Test Topic Alert!**

Keep in mind the distinction between federal covered securities, securities exempt from registration by the states because they are covered by federal legislation, and SEC-registered securities. SEC-registered securities are publicly held securities that trade interstate but are not listed on SEC-registered exchanges.

Registration by Coordination

A security may be **registered by coordination** if a registration statement has been filed under the Securities Act of 1933 in connection with the same offering.

In coordinating a federal registration with state registration, issuers must supply the following records in addition to the consent of service of process:

- copy of the latest form of prospectus filed under the Securities Act of 1933 if the Administrator requires;
- copy of articles of incorporation and bylaws, a copy of the underwriting agreement, or a specimen copy of the security;
- if the Administration requests, copies of any other information filed by the issuer under the Securities Act of 1933; and
- each amendment to the federal prospectus promptly after it is filed with the Securities and Exchange Commission.

Effective Date Registration by coordination becomes effective at the same time the federal registration becomes effective, provided the following conditions are met:

- no stop orders have been issued and no proceedings are pending against the issuer;
- registration has been on file for at least the minimum number of days specified by the Administrator, a number that currently ranges from 10 to 20 days, depending on the state; and
- statement of the maximum and minimum offering prices and underwriting discounts must be on file for two business days.

Registration by coordination is by far the most frequently used method.

Registration by Qualification

Any security can be **registered by qualification**. Registration by qualification requires a registrant to supply any information required by the state securities Administrator. Securities not eligible for registration by another method must be registered by qualification. In addition, securities that will be sold only in one state (intrastate) will be registered by qualification.

To register by qualification, an issuer must supply a consent to service of process and the following information.

- Name, address, form of organization, description of property, and nature of business
- Information on directors and officers and every owner of 10% or more of the issuers securities, and the remuneration paid to owners in the last 12 months
- Description of issuers' capitalization and long-term debt

- Estimated proceeds and the use to which the proceeds will be put
- Type and amount of securities offered, offering price, and selling and underwriting costs
- Stock options to be created in connection with the offering
- Copy of any prospectus, pamphlet, circular, or sales literature to be used in the offering
- Specimen copy of the security along with opinion of counsel as to the legality of the security being offered
- Audited balance sheet current within four months of the offering with an income statement for three years prior to date of the balance sheet

✓ **Take Note:** The Administrator may require additional information by rule or order. The Administrator may require that a prospectus be sent to purchasers prior to the sale, and that newly established companies register their securities for the first time in a state by qualification.

Effective Date Unlike coordination, where the effective date is triggered by SEC acceptance of the registration, a registration by qualification becomes effective whenever the state Administrator so orders. Registration is good for one year from that date.

✎ **Quick Quiz 2.3**

True or False?

____ 1. Simus Shoe Company, a new retail shoe store chain, has applied for the registration of its securities with the SEC as required by the Securities Act of 1933 and wants to register its securities in the state of Illinois. Simus would most likely register by coordination.

____ 2. Any company may register by qualification whether or not it files a statement with the SEC.

Answers

1. **T.** *Registration by coordination involves coordinating a state registration with that of a federal registration.*

2. **T.** *Any company may register by qualification. Companies that are not established or that intend to offer their securities in one state register by qualification.*

Exemptions from Registration

In certain situations, the USA exempts securities and transactions from registration and filing requirements of sales literature. A security, a transaction, or both, can be exempt.

Exempt Securities and Exempt Transactions

An **exempt security** retains its exemption when initially issued and in subsequent trading. However, an **exempt transaction** must be established before each transaction. The two are not mutually exclusive.

✓ **For Example:** A transaction can be exempt, but the security involved in that transaction may have to be registered. This is discussed later in the unit.

The Uniform Securities Act provides for a number of categories of exempt securities and even more categories of exempt transactions. Those securities that are **nonexempt** must register either by coordination or qualification. Certain federal covered securities do not register with the Administrator but file a notice with the Administrator. As mentioned above, an **exempt security** retains its exemption upon its initial issue as well as in subsequent trading.

An exemption for a transaction, on the other hand, must be established with each transaction. Provided it is in the public interest, the state Administrator can deny, suspend, or revoke any securities transaction exemption other than that of a federal covered security.

An **exempt security** is exempt from state registration. Most securities are exempt because they are issued by a government or regulated by the federal government or a regulatory agency. The purpose of the USA is to protect the public from fraudulent securities activities. NSMIA eliminated the dual registration of securities; if the federal government or regulatory agency regulates a security, states may not regulate these also, therefore the securities are exempt from state regulation under the USA.

✓ **Take Note:** A security is exempt due to the nature of the issuer, not the purchaser.

An **exempt transaction** is exempt from the regulatory control of the state Administrator because of the manner in which a sale is made or because of the person to whom the sale is made. A transaction is an action and must be judged by the merits of each instance.

The USA prohibits the sale of securities in the state unless they are registered in the state, exempt from registration in the state, or subject to an exempt transaction.

✓ **For Example:** A registered representative can sell a security that is not exempt in the state if the purchaser of the security is a bank or other institutional buyer. Because such sale is an exempt transaction, the sale can be made without registration. This means that the securities sold in exempt transactions do not have to be registered in the state. If such securities were not sold in exempt transactions, such as to an individual investor, they would have to be registered in the state.

Exempt Securities   Currently, there are 10 categories of securities exempt from registration and filing of sales literature requirements of the Uniform Securities Act.

1) United States Government and Municipal Securities. These include securities issued, insured or guaranteed by the United States, by a state, or by their political subdivisions.

2) Foreign Government Securities. These include securities issued, insured, or guaranteed by a foreign government (or any of their political subdivisions) with which the United States maintains diplomatic relations.

3) Depository Institutions and International Banks. These include securities that are issued, guaranteed by, or are a direct obligation of a depository institution or international bank (**depository institution** means bank, savings institution, or trust companies organized under the laws of the state).

4) Insurance Company Securities. These include securities issued, insured, or guaranteed by an insurance company authorized to do business in the state. Insurance companies securities refers to the stocks or bonds of insurance companies, not the policies issued by the companies. Fixed insurance and annuity policies are not securities so there is nothing to be exempt.

5) Public Utility Securities. These include any security issued or guaranteed by a railroad, other common carriers, public utility, or public utility holding company registered under the Public Holding Company Act of 1935; regulated as to rates by federal or state authority; or regulated in respect to issuance or guarantee of the security by a governmental authority of the United States, any state, Canada, or any Canadian province.

6) Certain Options and Rights. These include put or call option contracts, warrants, or subscription rights on a federal covered security. Also exempt under this category are options on a security, an index of securities, or foreign currency option issued by a clearing agency registered under the Securities Exchange Act of 1934.

7) Securities Issued by Nonprofit Organizations. These include securities issued by religious, educational, fraternal, charitable, social, athletic, reformatory, or trade associations.

8) Securities Issued by Cooperatives. These include securities issued by a nonprofit membership cooperative to members of that cooperative.

9) Securities of Employee Benefit Plans. This includes any investment contract issued by an employee stock purchase, saving, pension, or profit-sharing plan.

10) Equipment Trust Certificates. Equipment trust certificates issued on leased property by exempt or federal covered issuers. Exemptions from registration extend to **federal covered securities** or those securities listed on the New York Stock Exchange, the American Exchange, the Nasdaq National Market (NNM), and other regional stock exchanges.

✔ *Take Note:* Federal covered exemptions are known as **blue-chip exemptions**.

✔ *For Example:* Shares of investment companies registered under the Investment Company Act of 1940 are exempt as federal covered securities.

Under NSMIA, there cannot be dual coverage. However, federal covered securities can be required to pay filing fees to the states in which they are sold.

✔ *Take Note:* A promissory note (commercial paper), draft, bill of exchange, or banker's acceptance that matures within nine months, is issued in denominations of at least $50,000, and receives one of the three highest ratings by a nationally recognized rating agency is a federal covered security and also exempt from registration requirements.

Quick Quiz 2.4

1. Which of the following securities are exempt from registration and advertising filing requirements under the USA?

   I. Shares of investment companies registered under the Investment Company Act of 1940
   II. Shares sold on the Nasdaq National Market System
   III. AAA-rated promissory notes of $100,000 that mature in 30 days
   IV. Shares sold on the New York Stock Exchange

   A. I only
   B. II and IV
   C. II, III, and IV
   D. I, II, III and IV

2. Which of the following securities is NOT exempt from the registration and advertising requirements of the USA?

   A. Shares of Commonwealth Edison, a public utility holding company
   B. Securities issued by the Carnegie Endowment for Peace
   C. Securities issued by the National Bank of Canada
   D. Variable annuity contract issued by Prudential Insurance Co.

Answers

1. **D.** All of the securities are federal covered securities and therefore not subject to the registration and advertising filing requirements of the USA.

2. **D.** Variable annuities (whose performance depends upon the securities in a segregated fund) are nonexempt, which means they are covered by the act and have to register. Shares in public utilities, charitable foundations, and foreign banking institutions as listed in Choices A, B, and C are included in our list of exempt securities.

Exempt Transactions

The Uniform Securities Act allows exemptions for 17 types of **exempt transactions**. Securities sold in exempt transactions are not subject to the filing or registration and advertising requirements of the act because of the manner in which they are sold.

1) Isolated Nonissuer Transactions. Isolated nonissuer transactions include secondary (nonissuer) transactions, whether effected through a broker or not, that occur **infrequently** (very few transactions per broker per year; the exact number varies by state). However, these usually do not involve securities professionals. In the same manner that individuals placing a "for sale by owner" sign on their front lawns do not need a real estate license, one individual selling stock to another in a one-on-one transaction is engaging in a transaction exempt from the oversight of the Administrator, because the issuer is not receiving any of the proceeds and the parties involved are not trading as part of a regular practice.

2) Specified Nonissuer Transactions. These include nonissuer transactions by a registered agent, provided that the security has been outstanding in the public's hands for at least 90 days, and that the issuer has:

- a class of securities registered under the Securities Exchange Act of 1934;
- a class of securities registered under the Investment Company Act of 1940; or
- filed and maintained information comparable to that required under the Securities Exchange Act of 1934 with the Administrator for 180 days.

3) Foreign Nonissuer Transactions. These include nonissuer transactions in securities subject to the Securities Exchange Act of 1934 reporting requirements.

4) Nonissuer Transactions in Securities Subject to Securities Exchange Act Reporting. A nonissuer transaction in an outstanding security is exempt if the issuer files reports with the SEC.

5) Nonissuer Transactions in Specified Fixed-Income Securities. Issuers must not be in default nor in the organization stage in order for the transaction to be exempt.

6) Unsolicited Brokerage Transactions. These include transactions initiated by the client, not the agent. This is probably the most common of the exempt transactions.

7) Nonissuer Transactions by Pledgees. A nonissuer transaction executed by a bona fide pledgee (the one who received the security as collateral for a loan), as long as it was not for the purpose of evading the act.

Test Topic Alert!

These first seven transaction exemptions are available only for nonissuer transactions. An issuer selling securities in a primary or secondary offering may not rely on these exemptions.

8) Underwriter Transactions. These include transactions between issuer and underwriter as well as those between underwriters themselves.

9) Unit Secured Transactions. These include transactions in a bond backed by a real mortgage or deed of trust provided that the entire mortgage or deed of trust is sold as a unit.

10) Bankruptcy, Guardian, or Conservator Transactions. Transactions by an executor, administrator, sheriff, or trustee in bankruptcy are exempt transactions.

11) Institutional Investor Transactions. These are primarily financial institutions.

Test Topic Alert!

Remember the distinction between an **accredited investor** and **institutional investor**. An **accredited investor** is an investor who meets the accredited investor standards of Regulation D. Reg D standards require that an individual have a net worth greater than $1,000,000 or $200,000 in income for the last two years and the current year, invests for his own account, and has requisite knowledge to evaluate investments. This term only applies to federal law, not the USA, and will probably never be the correct answer to a USA question.

An **institutional investor** is an investor that manages large amounts of money for other people, such as a mutual fund, an insurance company, or a pension fund.

12) Limited Offering Transactions. These include any offering, called a **private placement**, directed at not more than 10 persons other than institutional investors during the previous 12 consecutive months, provided that:

- the seller believes that all of the non-institutional buyers are purchasing for investment purposes only;
- no commissions or other remuneration is paid for soliciting non-institutional investors; and
- no general solicitation or advertising is used.

Unlike federal law where the private placement rule restricts the number of purchasers, the USA restricts the number of offers that may be made.

13) Transactions with Existing Security Holders. No commissions may be paid. A transaction made under an offer to existing security holders of the issuer (including persons who are holders of convertible securities, rights or warrants) as long as no commission or other form of remuneration is paid directly or indirectly for soliciting that security holder.

14) Control Transactions. This includes mergers, consolidations, or reorganization transactions to which the issuer and the other person or its parent or subsidiary are parties.

15) Rescission Offers. These include offers made to rescind an improper transaction.

16) Out-of-State Offers or Sales. This includes an offer or sale of a security to a person who is not a resident of the state and is not present in the state.

17) Pre-Organization Certificates. An offer or sale of a pre-organization certificate or subscription is exempt, if it meets all of the following conditions:

- no commission or other renumeration is paid or given directly or indirectly for soliciting any subscriber;
- the number of subscribers does not exceed 10; and
- no payment is made by any subscriber.

The Administrator's Powers

The USA grants the Administrator the authority, by rule or order, to exempt a security, transaction, or offer from the USA's registration and filing requirements. In addition, the Administrator may waive a requirement for an exemption of a transaction or security.

✔ *For Example:* Securities and transactions that are exempt from the filing and advertising provisions of the Uniform Securities Act are not exempt from the antifraud provisions of state securities law.

The Administrator may, by rule or order, deny or revoke any exemption with respect to a security or transaction, other than that of a federal covered security, upon prior notice to the interested parties. The Administrator must also provide an opportunity for a hearing within 15 days of a written request. The Administrator also has the power to summarily deny or revoke exemptions pending final determination of any proceedings.

Under the Uniform Securities Act, the burden of providing an exemption or an exception from a definition falls upon the person claiming it.

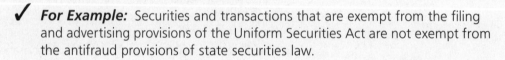

✏ Quick Quiz 2.5   Indicate an exempt transaction with **Y** and a non-exempt transaction with **N**.

 1. A nonissuer transaction in a security issued by a foreign government is an exempt transaction.

 2. Mr. Thompson, an agent with First Securities Inc. (a broker/dealer) receives an unsolicited request to purchase a security for Mary Gordon, a high net worth individual.

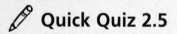 3. The sale of an unregistered security in a private, non-publicly advertised transaction, offered to 10 or fewer investors over the last 12 months.

 4. The sale of unclaimed securities by the Administrator of securities for the state of New Mexico.

 5. Sale of stock of a privately owned company to the public in an initial public offering.

No reg.

6. Which of the following are exempt transactions?

   I. A nonissuer transaction in a security issued by a foreign government with which the United States has diplomatic relations

   II. An unsolicited request from an existing client to purchase a non-exempt security

   III. The sale of an unregistered security in a private, non-publicly advertised transaction to 10 non-institutional purchasers over a period not exceeding 12 months

   IV. The sale of unlisted securities by a trustee in bankruptcy

   A. I, II, III and IV
   B. I, II and III only
   C. I, II and IV only
   D. I and II only

Answers

1. **Y.** *A nonissuer transaction in a foreign government issue is an exempt transaction.*

2. **Y.** *Mr. Thompson's receipt of an unsolicited order from Ms. Gordon is an exempt transaction.*

3. **Y.** *The sale of an unregistered security in a private, non-publicly advertised transaction to 10 or fewer offerees over the last 12 months is an exempt transaction (a private placement).*

4. **Y.** *The sale of unclaimed securities by the Administrator of securities for the state of New Mexico is an exempt transaction.*

5. **N.** *The sale of stock of a privately owned company to the public in an initial public offering is not an exempt transaction.*

must be reg

6. **C.** *The reason that Choice III is not an exempt transaction is that the private placement exemption is limited to 10 offerees, not 10 purchasers. The Administrator would be suspicious of anyone with a 100% closing ratio. All of the others are included in our list of exempt transactions.*

Securities HotSheet

Investment Contract (Howey Decision):
- Investment of money
- Common enterprise
- Expectation of profits
- Solely from efforts of others

Nonexempt Security:
- Must register

exempt

No register

Issuer:	• Company, government, or government subdivision that offers or proposes to offer securities
Nonissuer:	• Secondary market transaction • Proceeds do not go to issuer
Primary Offering:	• Initial public offering and any subsequent offering of new securities
Methods of Registration:	• Coordination, qualification
Notice Filing:	• Federal covered investment company securities—file documents with states
Exempt Security:	• No registration under USA required • Look at who the issuer is • Still subject to antifraud provisions
Exempt Transaction:	• Transaction need not be registered under USA • Look at who the purchaser is or how the trade is made

Series 63
Unit Test 2

1. Which of the following is defined as a security under the Uniform Securities Act?

   A. A guaranteed, lump-sum payment to a beneficiary
   B. Fixed, guaranteed payments made for life or for a specified period
   C. Commodity futures contracts
   D. An investment contract

2. Under the Uniform Securities Act, which of the following persons is responsible for proving that a securities issue is exempt from registration?

   A. Underwriter
   B. Issuer
   C. State Administrator
   D. There is no need to prove eligibility for an exemption.

3. Registration is effective when ordered by the Administrator in the case of registration by

   A. coordination
   B. integration
   C. notice filing
   D. qualification

4. The United States Supreme Court in the Howey decision ruled that an instrument that represents the investment of money in a common enterprise with an expectation of profit solely through the managerial efforts of others is a security. In following the Howey decision, the USA would consider which of the following a security?

   A. Purchase of a house in a desirable real estate market with the expectation that the house will be resold at a profit within a few years
   B. Purchase of jewelry for speculative purposes as opposed to personal use
   C. Investment in options to acquire a security
   D. Investment in commodities futures

5. Under the Uniform Securities Act, which of the following would be considered an exempt transaction?

   I. An existing client calls you to purchase 1,000 shares of a common stock that is not registered in this state
   II. The sale to an individual client of shares that are part of a registered secondary of a NYSE-listed company
   III. Shares of a bank's IPO are sold to an institutional client
   IV. Shares of an insurance company's IPO are sold to an individual client

   A. I and III only
   B. II and IV only
   C. I, III and IV only
   D. I, II, III and IV

6. Which of the following securities is(are) exempt from the registration provisions of the USA?

   I. Issue of a savings and loan association
   II. General obligation municipal bond
   III. Bond issued by a company that has common stock listed on the American Stock Exchange

   A. I only
   B. II only
   C. II and III only
   D. I, II and III

7. A primary issue is

   A. the first transaction between two parties in the over-the-counter market
   B. a sale between investors of securities traded on the New York Stock Exchange
   C. a new offering of an issuer purchased by an investor
   D. a secondary market transaction in a security recently offered to the public

8. All of the following describe exempt transactions EXCEPT

   A. ABC, a broker/dealer, purchases securities from XYZ corporation
   B. First National Bank sells its entire publicly-traded bond portfolio to Amalgamated National Bank
   C. Amalgamated Nation Bank sells its publicly traded bond portfolio to ABC Insurance Company
   D. Joe Smith, an employee of Amalgamated Bank, buys securities from ABC Brokerage Corporation

9. Under the USA, all of the following are exempt securities EXCEPT

   I. US government securities
   II. unsolicited transactions
   III. transactions between issuers and underwriters
   IV. securities of credit unions

   A. I, II and IV only
   B. I and IV only
   C. II and III only
   D. IV only

10. Registration statements for securities under the Uniform Securities Act are effective for

    A. a period of time determined by the Administrator for each issue
    B. one year from the effective date
    C. one year from the date of issue
    D. one year from the previous January 1

11. Under the Uniform Securities Act, an issuer is any person who issues, or proposes to issue, a security for sale to the public. According to the USA, which of the following is not an issuer?

    I. The city of Chicago, which is involved in a distribution of tax-exempt highway improvement bonds
    II. A partner in the AAA Oil and Gas Partnership sells his interest in the investment
    III. The AAA Manufacturing Company, which proposes to offer shares to the public but has not completed the offering
    IV. The United States government, which proposes to offer Treasury bonds

    A. I only
    B. II only
    C. I, II and III only
    D. I, II and IV only

12. Which of the following transactions are exempt from registration under the USA?

    I. A trustee of a corporation in bankruptcy liquidates securities to satisfy debt holders
    II. An offer of a securities investment is directed to 10 persons in the state during a 12-month consecutive period
    III. An agent frequently engages in nonissuer transactions in unregistered securities in his own account
    IV. Agents for an entrepreneur offer preorganization certificates to less than 10 investors in the state for a modest commission

    A. I and II only
    B. I and IV only
    C. II and IV only
    D. I, III and IV only

13. Which of the following is/are primary transactions?

    I. John inherited securities of the XYZ Corporation from his father who, as a founder to the company, received the shares directly from the company as a result of stock options.
    II. John sold the securities he had inherited from his father to his neighbor, Peter, at the market price without charging a commission.
    III. John's father, a founder of XYZ corporation, purchased shares of XYZ directly from the corporation subsequent to its founding without paying a commission.
    IV. John purchased shares in XYZ Corporation in a third-market transaction.

    A. I only
    B. I and II only
    C. III only
    D. I, II, III and IV

14. XYZ Corporation has been in business for over 20 years. They need additional capital for expansion, and determine that a public offering in their home state and neighboring states is appropriate. Which method of securities registration would most likely be used to register this initial public offering?

    A. Coordination
    B. Notice filing
    C. Qualification
    D. Any of the above

15. Which of the following meet the USA's definition of an exempt transaction?

    I. Transactions by an executor of an estate
    II. Transactions with an investment company registered under the Investment Company Act of 1940
    III. An unsolicited sale of a Bulletin Board stock
    IV. Sale of a new issue to an individual customer

    A. I, II, III and IV
    B. I, II and III only
    C. I and II only
    D. IV only

Series 63
Unit Test 2
Answers & Rationale

1. D. Investment contracts are defined as a security under the Uniform Securities Act. In fact, the term is often used as a synonym for a security. A guaranteed, lump-sum payment to a beneficiary is an endowment policy excluded from the definition of a security. Fixed, guaranteed payments made for life or for a specified period are fixed annuity contracts not defined as securities. Commodity futures contracts and the commodities themselves are not securities. Remember it is much easier to remember what is not a security than what is.

2. B. The burden of proof for claiming eligibility for an exemption falls to the person claiming the exemption. In the event the registration statement was filed by someone other than the issuer (such as selling stockholders or broker/dealer) that person must prove the claim.

3. D. Registration by qualification is the only one of the registration methods where the Administrator sets the effective date. The effective date under registration by coordination is set by the SEC and notice filing is merely the filing of certain documents in order for the registrant to be able to offer securities in that state. Effectiveness is upon filing.

4. C. The investment in options is the only one of the choices that meets the definition of a security. It is an investment in a common enterprise with the expectation that the owner will profit as a result of the managerial efforts of others. The purchase of a house or jewelry is a purchase of a real asset or product that may result in a profit for the owner but not as a result of the managerial efforts of a third party. Commodities futures contracts are specifically excluded from the definition of a security. Note that options on

futures, however, are securities under the USA. Remember the items listed that are not securities.

5. A. Choice I describes an unsolicited transaction, probably the most common of the exempt transactions. Choice III and IV represent issuer transactions with the difference being that an issuer transaction with an institution is exempt while one with an individual is not. Choice II is not exempt as it is an issuer transaction and only nonissuer transactions in listed stocks are exempt.

6. D. The USA exempts from registration a number of different issues. Included in that group are securities issued by a bank or anything that looks like a bank (a savings and loan; a credit union). Securities issued by a governmental unit are always exempt. Securities listed on the American Stock Exchange are part of a group known as federal covered securities that also includes those listed on the New York Stock Exchange and Nasdaq National Market issues.

7. C. A primary transaction is a new offering of an issuer purchased by an investor. The first transaction between two investors in the over-the-counter market refers to a secondary transaction (the market between investors). A sale between investors of securities traded on the New York Stock Exchange is another example of a secondary transaction.

8. D. The purchase of securities from a broker/dealer by an employee of a bank is a nonexempt transaction—it is a sale of a security by a broker/dealer to a member of the public and is therefore not exempt. Transactions between brokers and issuers; transactions between banks; and transactions between banks and insurance companies are exempt because they are transactions between financial institutions. Exempt transactions are most often identified by who the transaction is with rather than what type of security is involved.

9. C. Both unsolicited transactions and transactions between issuers and underwriters are exempt transactions, not exempt securities. US government securities and securities of credit

unions are exempt securities, not exempt transactions.

10. B. Securities registration statements are effective for one year from the effective date.

11. B. Under the Uniform Securities Act, an issuer is any person who issues, or proposes to issue, a security. Examples of issuers are a municipality such as the city of Chicago, which issues tax-exempt highway improvement bonds; the AAA Manufacturing Company, which proposes to offer shares to the public even though it has not completed the offering; and the United States government, when it proposes to offer Treasury bonds. Oil, gas, and mining partnerships are not issuers under the terms of the Uniform Securities Act; however, certificates of interest in them are securities. The resale of a partnership interest by an investor is a nonissuer sale because the investor is not the issuer.

12. A. Transactions by fiduciaries, such as a trustee in a bankruptcy reorganization, are exempt from registration. An offer of a securities investment to 10 or fewer persons (called a private placement) is also exempt from registration. Engaging in nonissuer transactions on a regular basis is not exempt from registration. That exemption is only granted in the case of isolated transaction, the opposite of regular. Offers of pre-

organization certificates are not exempt when commissions are charged.

13. C. A primary transaction is one where the issuer of the securities receives the proceeds of the sale. John's father, although a founder of the company, purchased shares *directly* from the company. This transaction is a primary transaction because the firm received the funds from the sale of the shares. In all the other instances, the firm, the original issuer of the securities, did not receive the proceeds of the transaction. These transactions are called nonissuer transactions.

14. A. Since this offering is being made in more than one state, SEC registration is necessary; the state registration method would be coordination, which is the simultaneous registration of a security with both the SEC and the states.

15. B. Transactions by a fiduciary, such as the executor of an estate, are included in the definition of exempt transaction. So are transactions with certain institutional clients like investment companies and insurance companies. The Bulletin Board is an electronic medium for the trading of highly speculative, thinly capitalized issues. Because the order is an unsolicited one the transaction is exempt. Sale of a new issue of stock to an individual client would not be an exempt transaction.

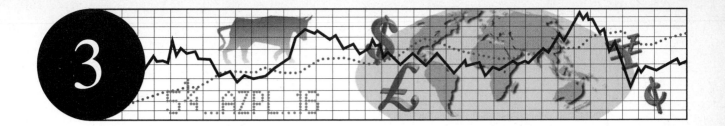

Unethical Business Practices

INTRODUCTION

The Uniform Securities Act was drafted to eliminate conflicts in various state securities legislation and to protect the public from fraudulent securities practices. Courts and self-regulatory agencies have determined those activities that are fraudulent. The securities industry has developed standards of ethics and fair practice that all securities professionals must follow to avoid fraud and to conduct business in an ethical manner.

This unit discusses practices which are fraudulent under the USA as well as those that, while they do not constitute fraud, are prohibited by law or by the rules of the Administrator or **self-regulatory organizations** (SROs) within the securities industry.

Fraudulent and prohibited practices are the most heavily tested topics, and you must know what these practices are and be able to apply the principles that guide ethical behavior in specific situations.

Fraudulent and prohibited practices make up 35% of the exam. The Series 63 exam will include approximately 21 questions on the material presented in this unit.

Appendix B, which contains NASAA's statements of policy on "Dishonest or Unethical Business Practices by Broker/Dealers and Agents in Connection with Investment Company Shares," "Unethical Business Practices of Investment Advisers," and "Dishonest or Unethical Business Practices of Broker/Dealers and Agents" are an integral part of this unit. Study them carefully both in connection with this unit and as a review for your exam.

UNIT OBJECTIVES   When you have completed this unit, you should be able to:

- describe the antifraud provisions of the USA;
- recognize specific fraudulent and prohibited practices;
- make distinctions between prohibitions that pertain to sales of securities and those that pertain to the sale of investment advice;
- list the required provisions for investment advisory contracts; and
- identify various types of market manipulation.

The Antifraud Provisions of the USA

Our system of laws is derived from the old British Common Law and there are certain terms that have an everyday common meaning. The legal definition of fraud is: "not limited to common law deceit." The Uniform Securities Act has a specific definition of fraud. The USA asserts that, in addition to what is ordinarily considered a fraudulent practice, there are others that come under the act. Fraud must be willful or done knowingly. There is no such thing as accidental fraud.

Fraudulent activity may occur when conducting sales or purchases of securities and when providing investment advice. Each of these categories is discussed separately.

Fraudulent & Prohibited Practices in the Sale of Securities

Under the USA, it is unlawful for any person, when engaged in the offer, sale, or purchase of any security, directly or indirectly, to:

- employ any device, scheme, or artifice to defraud;
- make any untrue statement of a material fact or omit to state a material fact necessary to make a statement not misleading; or
- engage in any act, practice, or course of business that operates as a fraud or deceit upon a person.

✓ **Take Note:** There are no exceptions to the anti-fraud provisions of the act. They apply to any person and any securities transaction whether registered, exempt, or federal covered.

While the USA does not list the prohibited practices, the following have been held by courts, regulatory agencies, and state Administrators to be fraudulent, dishonest, or unethical practices and therefore prohibited. These include the following:

- Misleading or untrue statements
- Failure to state material facts
- Using inside information
- Making unsuitable investment recommendations
- Exercising discretion without previous written authority
- Borrowing money or securities from chests
- Commingling customer funds and securities
- Guaranteeing client profits
- Sharing in client accounts
- Market manipulation

✓ **Take Note:** All such practices are prohibited, whether they are fraudulent or not.

Misleading or Untrue Statements

The USA prohibits any person from making any **misleading** or **untrue statements of material fact** in connection with the purchase or sale of a security. Not all facts are material. The law defines **material** as information that is used by a prospective purchaser to make an investment decision.

✓ **For Example:** If the company's address were incorrect, that would not generally be considered an <u>untrue statement</u> of a material fact because it is highly unlikely that an investor makes an investment decision based upon the company's street address. On the other hand, misstating the qualifications of the CEO would be material because investors do look at the management of the enterprise when making an investment decision.

The following are examples of untrue statements of material fact that constitute fraud if made knowingly and willfully.

- **Inaccurate market quotations**—telling a client the stock is up when the reverse is true is obviously an improper action. However, it would not be considered fraud if the inaccuracy was due to a malfunction of the quote machine or an unintended clerical error. To be considered fraud, the action must be deliberate.
- **Misstatements of an issuer's earnings or projected earnings or dividends**—telling a client that earnings are up, or that the dividend will be increased when such is not the case, is clearly a fraudulent action. It would not be fraud if you were quoting a news release that was incorrect.
- **Inaccurate statements as to the amount of commissions, markup, or markdown**—there are circumstances where the amount of commission or markup may be higher than normal. That is permissible, as long as properly disclosed. But telling a client that it costs him nothing to trade with your firm because you never charge a commission, and not informing him that all trades are done on a principal basis with a markup or markdown, is fraud.
- **Telling a customer that a security will be listed on an exchange without concrete information concerning its listing status**—years ago, before the days of Nasdaq National Market securities, an announcement that a stock was going to be listed on the NYSE invariably caused

its market price to jump. Even though it doesn't have the same significance today (a better example would be a Nasdaq SmallCap market stock going NNM), any statement of this type relating to a change in marketplace for the security is only permitted if, in fact, you have knowledge that such change is imminent.

- **Informing a client that the registration of a security with the SEC or with the state securities Administrator means that the security has been approved by these regulators**—registration never implies approval.

- **Misrepresenting the status of customer accounts**—This behavior is fraudulent. Many people are not motivated to pay strict attention to their monthly account statements, making it relatively easy for an unscrupulous agent to fraudulently claim increasing values in the account when the opposite is true. Doing so would be a clearly fraudulent action.

- **Promising a customer services without any intent to perform them or without being properly qualified to perform them**—You say, "yes I can" to your client, even if you know you can't deliver. For instance, the client asks you to analyze her bond portfolio to determine the average duration. Even though you don't know how to do that, you agree to do so. Under the USA, you have just committed fraud.

- **Representing to customers that the Administrator approves of the broker/dealer or agent's abilities**—this is another case of using the word *approve* improperly. A broker/dealer or agent is registered, not approved.

✓ **Take Note:** Merely learning the terms is not always enough to get you through the exam. It's being able to apply the knowledge that is critical to success. The following case studies cover many of the fraudulent and prohibited practices.

Case Study: Making Leading or Untrue Statements

Situation: Mr. Thompson, a registered securities agent in Illinois, informs a long-standing client, Ms.Gordon, that her largest equity holding, First Tech Internet Services, Inc., will be listed on the New York Stock Exchange upon completion of its application for listing. In addition, he exaggerates the earnings by $1.00 per share to make her more comfortable and encourage her to buy more shares. Thompson is convinced the earnings will rise to that amount and does not want Ms. Gordon to sell because he believes the stock will appreciate in price once listed on the exchange. He also tells her that, due to the fact that his firm will not be charging her any commission on the trade as they already have the stock in inventory, she will be ahead from the start.

Analysis: Mr. Thompson violated the USA by deliberately misrepresenting the earnings of First Tech Internet Services. Although Mr. Thompson's motives may have been good, he must be truthful in his effort to encourage clients to purchase more stock—his conviction that stock would rise upon its listing on the NYSE is not sufficient. No violation of the act occurred with respect to First Tech's exchange listing because Mr. Thompson knew that the stock was in registration to be listed on the NYSE. Stating that the firm will not charge a commission, but failing to state that a sale from inventory would include a markup, is a fraudulent act.

In addition to the fraudulent practices listed above, there are a number of other prohibited business practices relating to the sale and purchase of securities.

Failure to State Material Facts

The USA does not require an agent to provide all information about an investment, only that information that is **material** to making an informed investment decision. However, the agent must not fail to mention material information that could have an impact of the price of the security. In addition, the agent may not state facts that in and of themselves are not untrue but, as a result of deliberately omitting others, renders the recommendation misleading under the circumstances.

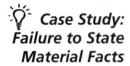

Case Study: Failure to State Material Facts

Situation: Upon acceptance of the listing application by the NYSE, there is an announcement that First Tech Internet Services will publish its financial statements in a newspaper ad. Mr. Thompson deliberately failed to mention this advertisement to Ms. Gordon.

After its listing on the New York Stock Exchange, the research department in Mr. Thompson's firm prepares a very negative report on First Tech. The research department discovered a change in accounting practices that will have a detrimental affect on subsequent earnings reported by First Tech. Mr. Thompson continues to recommend the stock to Ms. Gordon because he believes the increased exposure gained by the exchange listing will outweigh the future decline in earnings. As a result, Thompson neglects to inform Ms. Gordon of the change prior to her purchase of additional shares.

Analysis: Mr. Thompson violated the USA even though he made no misleading statements to Ms. Gordon with respect to First Tech. Mr. Thompson did not have to mention the ad in the paper because it is not material, yet he violated the act when he failed to mention the accounting change that would result in significantly lower earnings. Although an accounting change is not ordinarily a material fact, in this case it was because it would have a detrimental impact on the company's earnings and its market price.

Using Inside Information

Making recommendations based on **material inside information** about an issuer or its securities is prohibited. Should an agent come into possession of inside information, the agent must report the possession of the information to a supervisor or compliance officer.

 Take Note: Material inside information under securities law is any information about a company that has not been communicated to the general marketplace and that would likely have an impact on the value of a security.

Case Study: Using Inside Information

Situation: Mr. Thompson is a friend and neighbor of Mr. Cage, president and owner of more than half of First Tech's securities. Mr. Cage discloses to Mr. Thompson that the company has just discovered a new technology that will double First Tech's earnings within the next year. No one outside of the company, except for Mr. Thompson, knows of this discovery. On this basis, Mr. Thompson buys additional shares of First Tech for Ms. Gordon.

Analysis: The information on First Tech's new technology is material inside information that has not been made public. It is material information that only Mr. Thompson and company officials know. Mr. Thompson violated the USA in acting upon this information. Mr. Thompson should have communicated the possession of the information to his compliance officer and refrained from making recommendations on the basis of this information.

Making Unsuitable Investment Recommendations

Agents must always have reasonable grounds for making recommendations to clients. Prior to making recommendations, the agent must inquire into the client's financial status, investment objectives, and ability to assume financial risk.

The following practices violate the suitability requirements under the USA as well as the rules of fair practice that regulatory agencies have developed. A securities professional may not:

- recommend securities transactions without regard to customer financial situation, needs, or investment objectives;
- induce transactions solely to generate commissions (churning) defined as transactions in customer accounts that are excessive in size or frequency, in relation to the client's financial resources or the character of the account;
- recommend a security without reasonable grounds;
- fail to sufficiently describe the important facts and risks concerning a transaction or security.

Case Study: Making Unsuitable Investment Recommendations

Situation: Mr. Thompson has a wide variety of clients: high net worth individuals, trusts, and retirees with limited incomes and resources, and college students. Mr. Thompson has strong beliefs about First Tech, a growth stock that pays no dividends. He forcefully recommends the stock to all his clients without informing them of the volatility of First Tech and the research department's pending downgrade in earnings. He also informs his clients of the new technology breakthrough that Mr. Cage, the president of First Tech, had told him in confidence.

Analysis: Mr. Thompson has violated the USA on several counts. First, he made a recommendation without regard to the separate financial conditions, needs, and objectives of his diverse client base. The recommendation is unsuitable for the investment objectives of his retired clients with fixed incomes and limited financial resources. Additionally, he made the recommendation in an unsuitable manner by failing to reveal the earnings volatility or risk and the downgrade in earnings—and then he revealed inside information to clients while making recommendations based on that information.

Exercising Discretion Without prior Written Authority

Registered representatives of broker/dealers may not exercise discretion in an account without **prior written authority (power of attorney)** from the client. Prior written authority is also known as **trading authorization**.

Discretion is given to the firm and authorizes the firm to decide the:

- **a**sset (what security);
- **a**ction (buy or sell); and
- **am**ount (how many shares).

However, merely authorizing the firm to determine the best price or time to trade is not considered to be discretion.

Case Study: Discretionary Trading Authorization

Situation: Mr. Thompson's client, Mr. Bixby, has indicated over the phone that he authorizes Mr. Thompson to make trades for him. Mr. Bixby's family lawyer, Mr. Derval, has specific power of attorney over some of Mr. Bixby's businesses. Mr. Bixby promised Mr. Thompson that he would send in the trading authorization within the next day or two to give Thompson discretion over the account. However, Mr. Thompson immediately executes trades in First Tech for Mr. Bixby to take advantage of its impending NYSE listing.

The following week, Mr. Thompson receives Mr. Bixby's written discretionary trading authorization. On the day after the authorization arrived, Mr. Bixby's attorney, Mr. Derval, indicates that Mr. Bixby would like to buy shares in General Electric. Because Mr. Derval has power of attorney for Mr. Bixby, Mr. Thompson bought the shares.

Analysis: Mr. Thompson violated the USA by trading in Mr. Bixby's account prior to receipt of the written trading authorization. Having authorization "in the mail" is not sufficient. Mr. Thompson also violated the USA by accepting the order from Mr. Derval because although he is Bixby's attorney, he was not specifically authorized to trade in Mr. Bixby's securities account. The trading authorization signed by Mr. Bixby only gave authority to Mr. Thompson. Had Mr. Derval provided Thompson with specific written third-party trading authorization from Mr. Bixby, Mr. Thompson then could have accepted the order for General Electric without a violation of the act.

✓ **Take Note:** If Mr. Thompson is an investment adviser representative working for an investment adviser, he may exercise discretionary authority without obtaining written authority for 10 days after the date of the first transaction.

Borrowing Money or Securities from Clients

Securities professionals may not borrow money or client securities for their personal use unless that person is a bank or securities firm in the business of lending money and/or securities.

💡 Case Study: Borrowing Money or Securities from Clients

Situation: On occasion, Mr. Thompson borrows cash from his discretionary client, Mr. Bixby, when Mr. Bixby's account is not fully invested. Mr. Bixby has given Mr. Thompson much latitude because Mr. Thompson has done well in managing the account and Mr. Thompson always repays the money in time to reinvest Mr. Bixby's funds in new securities purchases. Thompson justifies these borrowings as within the discretionary power Mr. Bixby had granted him. The First National Bank is also a client of Mr. Thompson, but he does not borrow from the bank because it charges unusually high interest rates.

Analysis: Mr. Thompson has engaged in a prohibited practice because securities professionals may not borrow from customers who are not banks. Furthermore, Mr. Thompson violated the USA in exceeding the specific discretionary authority that Mr. Bixby had authorized. Mr. Bixby had authorized Mr. Thompson to trade in securities—not to take his money for personal use. Had Thompson decided to borrow from The First National Bank, that would have been permitted because they are an entity engaged in the business of lending money.

Commingling Customer Funds and Securities

Securities that are held in customer name must not be **commingled** (mixed) with those of the firm.

✓ **For Example:** If a firm has 100,000 shares of General Electric stock in its own proprietary account and its clients separately own an additional 100,000 shares, the firm may not place customer shares in the firm's proprietary account.

To mix shares together would give undue leverage or borrowing power to a firm and could jeopardize the security of client securities in the event of default.

Guaranteeing Client Profits

Securities professionals may not **guarantee** a certain performance, nor may they guarantee against a loss by providing funds to the account.

✓ **Take Note:** The term *guaranteed* under the USA means "guaranteed as to payment of principal, interest, or dividends." It is allowable to refer to a guaranteed security when an entity other than the issuer is making the guarantee. However, the regulatory agencies of the securities industry prohibit securities professionals from guaranteeing the performance returns of an investment or portfolio.

Sharing in Client Accounts

Agents cannot share in the profits or losses of client accounts unless the client and the broker/dealer supply prior written approval and the account is jointly owned. Furthermore, the gains and losses must be in proportion to the funds invested. In such a situation, it would be permissible to commingle the agent's and the customer's funds.

✓ **Take Note:** An agent and a customer can have a joint account in which they share profits and losses in proportion to the amount invested. However, clients and a broker/dealer cannot have joint accounts.

agent + customer   not client + B/d

Market Manipulation Securities legislation is designed to uphold the integrity of markets and transactions in securities. However, market integrity is violated when transactions misrepresent actual securities prices or market activity. The most common forms of market manipulation are **front running** and **matching purchases**.

Front running is the practice of entering an order for the benefit of a firm or a securities professional before entering customer orders.

 For Example: If a securities professional receives an order from an institutional client to purchase a large number of shares, the securities representative or firm cannot enter a personal order prior to completing the customer's purchase in an effort to benefit from a likely price rise.

Matched purchases occur when market participants agree to buy and sell securities among themselves to create the appearance of activity or trading in a security. Increased volume in a security can induce unsuspecting investors to purchase the security, thereby bidding up the price. As the price rises, those who initiated the matched purchases sell their securities at a profit.

 Take Note: **Arbitrage** is not a form of market manipulation; it is the simultaneous buying and selling of the same security in different markets to take advantage of different prices. Simultaneously buying a security in one market and selling it in another forces prices to converge and, therefore, provides uniform prices for the general public.

Other Prohibited Practices in the Sale of Securities

Security industry regulatory agencies prohibited a number of practices that violate industry standards of fair practice. Some of these prohibited practices follow.

- Deliberately failing to follow a customer's order
- Effecting transactions with customers not recorded on the books of the employing broker/dealer without express prior written consent
- Failing to bring written customer complaints to the attention of the employing broker/dealer
- Failing to inform customers that certain transactions involve larger than ordinary commissions, taxes, or transaction costs
- Soliciting orders for unregistered, nonexempt securities
- Spreading rumors
- Recommending transactions based on rumors
- Failure to disclose capacity (did the firm act as a broker or a dealer?) on a trade confirmation
- Dividing or otherwise splitting the agent's commissions for the purchase or sale of securities with any person not also registered as an agent for the same broker/dealer, or for an affiliated broker/dealer

- Backdating any records, including confirmations
- Attempting to obtain a written agreement for a customer that he/she will not sue the agent even though the sale of certain securities is in violation of state law. Any such agreement or waiver is not valid.

Case Study: Prohibited Practices—Trades Not on the Books

Situation: Mr. Thompson, a registered agent for First Securities, Inc., of Illinois, is also a part owner of Computer Resources Inc., a privately traded company in the state. Mr. Thompson is also a friend of Mr. Byers, the chairman of Aircraft Parts Inc., a large manufacturing company traded on the New York Stock Exchange. Mr. Byers has an account with Mr. Thompson at First Securities.

Mr. Thompson decides to sell his shares in Computer Resources to one of his clients. Since the shares are not publicly traded, Mr. Thompson completes the trades without informing First Securities or recording the transaction on their books. Mr. Thompson believes there is no need to inform his employer because the shares are privately traded. On the following day, Mr. Byers calls Mr. Thompson and indicates that he would like to sell his shares in Aircraft Parts. Mr. Thompson, who now has plenty of liquid assets from the sale of his shares in Computer Resources, decides to buy the shares directly from Mr. Byers. Mr. Thompson does not record the trade on the records of First Securities because he considers it a private transaction between himself and Mr. Byers.

Analysis: In both cases, Mr. Thompson has engaged in a prohibited practice. A registered agent may not conduct transactions with customers of his employing broker/dealer that are not recorded on the books without prior written consent. It makes no difference whether the shares Mr. Thompson sold were privately traded—when an agent effects trades with clients of the firm, they must be recorded on the books of the firm unless prior written authorization is obtained from the firm.

Case Study: Prohibited Practices—Customer Complaints and Front Running

Situation: Upon completion of the sale of his shares in Aircraft Parts, Inc., Mr. Byers has considerable funds to invest. Mr. Thompson then recommends to Byers that he purchase Simus Shoes, a thinly traded chain store that First Securities analysts have highly recommended subsequent to its initial public offering. Mr. Byers agrees. Just prior to entering Mr. Byers' orders, Mr. Thompson purchases several hundred shares for himself. Mr. Byers learned of Mr. Thompson's purchase and wrote him a stinging letter of complaint about it. Since Mr. Thompson considered the transaction a private matter, he did not think it necessary to bring the letter to the attention of First Securities. A few days later, Mr. Thompson personally apologized to Mr. Byers and took him out for a drink.

Analysis: Mr. Thompson has engaged in two practices that violate industry practice. First, while the recommendation of Simus Shoes was perfectly appropriate, it was not appropriate for Mr. Thompson to enter his personal order for the same shares prior to completing Mr. Byers' purchase. This is known as **front running,** a prohibited practice. Additionally, Mr. Thompson (as a registered agent) must bring all written complaints to the attention of his employer. Had Mr. Byers simply lodged a verbal complaint, Mr. Thompson would not have been under an obligation to bring it to the attention of the manager of his office. Taking Mr. Byers out for a drink did not violate industry standards.

✏️ **Quick Quiz 3.1**   Write **U** for unlawful or prohibited activities and **L** for lawful activities.

✓ u ___ 1. An agent guarantees a client that funds invested in mutual funds made up of government securities cannot lose principal.

sh L ___ 2. A non-discretionary customer calls his agent and places a buy order for 1,000 shares of any hot internet company. Later in the day, the representative enters an order for 1,000 shares of Global Internet Services.

✓ u L ___ 3. An agent receives a call from his client's spouse advising him to sell her husband's securities. Her husband is out of the country and requested that his wife call the agent. The agent refuses because the wife does not have trading authorization and she complains vigorously to his manager.

✓ u ___ 4. A client writes a letter of complaint to his agent regarding securities that the agent had recommended. The agent calls the client to apologize and then disposes of the letter because the client seemed satisfied.

✓ L ___ 5. A registered agent borrows $10,000 from a credit union that is one of her best customers.

✓ u ___ 6. An agent is convinced that Internet Resources will rise significantly over the next three months. She offers to buy the stock back from her customers at 10% higher than its current price at any time during the next three months.

✓ L ___ 7. An agent receives an order for the purchase of an obscure foreign security. The agent informs the client that the commissions and charges on this purchase will be much higher than those of domestic securities.

7/9 ✓ u ___ 8. A registered rep who works for a small broker that employs no securities analysts assures her clients that she can analyze any publicly traded security better than any analyst and that she will do it personally for each security purchased by a client, regardless of the industry.

L ___ 9. A securities sales agent recommends that her client buy 1,000 shares of Internet Consultants, Inc., an unregistered nonexempt security with a bright future.

Answers

1. **U.** *It is unlawful to guarantee the performance of any security. Government securities, although default-free, have interest rate risk or market price risk that an agent may not guarantee.*

2. **U.** *It is unlawful to exercise discretion without prior written authorization. Since the client was a non-discretionary client, the agent could not, on his own initiative, select which internet company to invest in.*

3. **L.** *An agent must refuse orders from anyone other than the customer unless that person has prior written trading authority.*

4. **U.** *All written customer complaints must be forwarded to a principal of the agent's employing broker/dealer.*

5. **L.** *Agents may borrow from banks or financial institutions that are in the business of lending money to public customers. Agents may not borrow money from their customers who are not in the business of lending money.*

6. **U.** *An agent may not guarantee the performance of a security.*

7. **L.** *It is lawful to charge extra transaction fees when justified as long as the customer is informed prior to the transaction.*

8. **U.** *It is unlawful to promise services that an agent cannot reasonably expect to perform or that the agent is not qualified to perform.*

9. **U.** *It is unlawful to solicit unregistered nonexempt securities.*

Fraudulent & Prohibited Practices When Providing Investment Advice

The fraudulent and prohibited practices described so far have related to the sale of securities. The Uniform Securities Act also prohibits fraudulent activities when providing investment advice.

The USA makes it unlawful for any person who receives compensation (directly or indirectly) for advising another person (whether through analyses or reports) as to the value of securities to employ any device, scheme, or artifice to defraud the other person. Additionally, they may not engage in any act, practice, or course of business which operates or would operate as a fraud or deceit upon the other person or engage in dishonest or unethical practices as the Administrator may define by rule.

✓ **Take Note:** Prohibitions are determined by the nature of the activity, not the registration status of the person engaged in the activity. Broker/dealers and their agents may give investment advice, yet not be included in the definition of investment adviser. It is also possible for investment advisers to be involved in the purchase and/or sale of securities. It is not who is doing the act, but the improper nature of the act that is important.

✓ **For Example:** An agent providing investment advice and an investment adviser engaged in selling are equally subject to the prohibitions against fraud.

Fiduciary Responsibility

When securities professionals act in an investment advisory capacity, they are called **fiduciaries** and are held to higher ethical standards than when they are engaged in the sales of securities. **Fiduciary responsibility** exceeds that which is normally required of ordinary business relationships because the fiduciary is in a position of trust. The fiduciary must act for the benefit of the client and place the interests of their clients above their own.

Investment advisers are paid for their advice. In the eyes of the law, that places them in a higher level of responsibility.

✓ **Take Note:** Investment advisers and their representatives are bound by the same restrictions as broker/dealers and their agents. In addition, investment advisers, as fiduciaries, must place the interests of their clients above those of their own, and advisers must have written investment advisory contracts with their clients (unless exempted by the Administrator). Those contracts must inform clients of fees and how they are computed and contain a prohibition against assignment (transfer) of the account without client permission.

Disclosure of Capacity

As a result of the fiduciary relationship that exists between an investment adviser and the client, the Uniform Securities Act places greater disclosure burdens on investment advisers. Prior to the entering of a transaction, an adviser must disclose to clients whether the firm is acting as a principal or broker in the transaction. This is in contrast to the rule for broker/dealers who only have to make this disclosure prior to the completion of the transaction, not in advance.

The USA acknowledges that it is not unusual for a broker/dealer to sell securities to a client from its inventory. In fact, that is what market makers do every day. But it would be unusual for an investment adviser to recommend a particular stock and then sell his own stock to the client. That is why prior notification and consent is necessary.

Agency Cross Transaction. An **agency cross transaction** is a transaction in which an adviser acts as an investment adviser as well as a broker/dealer for either or both sides. The adviser must disclose this capacity to clients and receive consent in writing prior to conducting the trade.

✓ *For Example:* An adviser has a client who is very conservative and another who generally looks for more aggressive positions. The conservative client calls and expresses concerns about the volatility of First Tech Internet Services, Inc., stating that he thinks this may be the best time to exit his position. The adviser agrees and mentions that he has a risk-taking client for whom First Tech is suitable and he'd like to "cross" the security between the two clients, charging a small commission to each of them. With the permission of both parties, this is not a violation.

✓ *Take Note:* In an agency cross transaction, the adviser may not recommend the transaction to both parties of the trade.

An exception to the prior written consent requirement is made when an investment adviser only provides what is called **impersonal investment advice.** This is typically the case with investment newsletters where the publisher discloses that they may have a position in the securities being recommended.

✓ *Take Note:* Impersonal investment advice is advice publicly distributed to 35, or more persons that does not purport to meet the objectives of specific individuals.

Investment Advisory Contracts

The primary relationship between a client and an investment adviser is determined by an **investment advisory contract.** The USA makes it unlawful for an investment adviser to enter into, extend, or renew any investment advisory contract unless in writing or the Administrator, by rule or order, provides otherwise.

All investment advisory contracts must state, in writing, that:

- the investment adviser shall not be compensated on the basis of a share in (percentage of) the capital appreciation of the client's funds;
- no investment advisory contract may be assigned to another adviser without the consent of the client; and
- if a partnership, the client shall be notified of any change in membership of the partnership within a reasonable time after the change.

Disclosure must be made of any material legal action in the past 10 years against the adviser at least 48 hours in advance of contracting with the client.

✓ *Take Note:* Pledging a majority interest in the adviser's stock as collateral for a loan is considered to be an assignment of the firm's advisory contracts. If the firm is organized as a partnership, a change in a minority interest requires notification while a change to a majority interest is the same as an assignment and requires consent.

✓ **Take Note:** It is required that an investment adviser must disclose any adverse financial condition that could impair the ability of the firm to perform its duties.

Investment Advisory Fees

The USA does not allow an investment adviser to share in a client's capital gains. The adviser is allowed to charge the client a fee based upon the total value of a fund averaged over a definite period (e.g., quarterly or annually). However, there are exceptions to this prohibition. An investment adviser is permitted to charge a performance-based fee to institutional clients and to individuals who meet one of the following two requirements:

- a minimum of $750,000 invested with the adviser; or
- a minimum net worth of $1,500,000.

 Case Study: Assignment and Notification of Change in Membership

Situation: Mr. Bixby withdrew $10 million from his account at the end of the year, leaving less than $750,000 under management with Market Tech Advisers, Inc., an advisory company incorporated in Illinois. During the course of the year, three officers left the firm. As a matter of corporate policy, Market Tech did not advise Mr. Bixby of these changes.

The following year, Market Tech (without notifying Mr. Bixby) assigned his account to Associated Investment Partners, a small partnership located in California, and Mr. Bixby was happy with the new partnership. Shortly after the assignment, Mr. Bixby learned of the death of one of the major partners through an article in the newspaper. He retained his account at Associated even though he had not been informed by them of the partner's death.

Analysis: Market Tech Advisers, Inc., was under no obligation to inform Mr. Bixby of the change in officers because it is a corporation and not a partnership. However they did violate the USA by assigning Mr. Bixby's account to Associated Partners without his consent. Additionally, the USA requires partnerships to inform clients of any change in partner membership within a reasonable amount of time after the change, which means that Associated Partners violated the USA by not informing Mr. Bixby of the partner's death.

Case Study: Investment Advisory Fees

Situation: Market Tech Advisers, a registered investment advisory company, charges clients a fee of 1% of their assets managed by the firm based upon the average amount of funds in the account each quarter. In addition, for some of their high net worth clients, Market Tech charges a fee based upon the degree to which their performance exceeds that of the S&P 500. Last quarter, Market Tech's performance was extremely good and, as a result, the fees of one of its largest clients, Mr. Bixby, more than doubled. Next quarter, the value of the account dropped by 25% and so did the fee. Mr. Bixby complained that Market Tech was sharing in his capital appreciation in violation of the USA, as he no longer had the required funds on deposit in the account.

Analysis: Market Tech is in compliance with the USA. Market Tech charged Mr. Bixby a 1% fee based upon the total assets in the account over a designated period as well as the stated performance fee. Since the assets increased and the performance beat the benchmark, so did the fee. Market Tech based its fees on the average value of funds under management and on a percentage of Mr. Bixby's capital gains—a practice in compliance with the USA for investors with a net worth at his level. Even though he no longer had $750,000 at the firm, his net worth was still in excess of $1.5 million. In the subsequent quarter, Market Tech's fee declined by 25% as a result of market deterioration. More than likely, there was no incentive fee earned in this quarter.

Custody of Client Funds and Securities

Under the USA, it is unlawful for an adviser to have custody of client funds and securities if:

- the Administrator in the state prohibits, by rule, advisers from having custody;
- in absence of a rule, an adviser fails to notify the Administrator that he has custody; and
- the adviser fails to supply clients, no less frequently than quarterly, with a statement of account activity and the location and amount of their assets.

Custody is the physical possession or control of funds and securities. Many advisers do not have custody because their client funds and securities are maintained at a bank or brokerage house. The adviser makes investment decisions under an advisory contract with the client's funds and securities placed in a custodial account at a commercial bank. Most Administrators will require those advisers who maintain custody to provide a surety bond or meet certain net worth standards.

 Take Note: The term **custody** does not include the use of discretion or advisory fees that represent prepayment.

There are several other prohibited practices of investment advisers that you must be familiar with.

- Disclosing the identity or investments of a client without consent of the client, unless required by law. An example of "forced" disclosure would be a subpoena to testify in a divorce case or a demand by the IRS to provide information about a client who is the subject of an audit.
- Using third-party prepared materials without proper attribution. Reports that are purely statistical in nature are excluded from this requirement, but a research report or market letter prepared by another entity could only be used if its authorship were disclosed.

- Use of any advertisement, (an ad is defined as a communication to more than one person) that uses any testimonial (NASD rules do not prohibit testimonials while the USA does). An advertisement may make reference to specific past performance of the adviser's recommendations as long as all recommendations of the same type of security for at least the past 12 months are included (not only the winners, but the losers as well).

Quick Quiz 3.2

1. An investment advisory contract need not include

   A. the fees and their method of computation
   B. a statement prohibiting assignment of client accounts without client consent
   C. the states in which the adviser is licensed to conduct business
   D. notification requirement upon change in membership if an investment partnership

   True or False?

2. An Administrator may not prevent custody of securities or funds if an adviser notifies the Administrator prior to taking custody.

3. An adviser may not sell securities to its customers from its own proprietary account.

4. Under USA antifraud provisions, an investment adviser is bound by the restrictions that apply to sales practices when engaged in sales activities.

Answers

1. **C.** The USA does not require investment advisers to include in their contracts a list of those states in which they are licensed to do business. The USA does require advisers to include their method of computing fees, a statement prohibiting assignment without client consent, and notification of change in membership of the investment partnership.

2. **F.** An Administrator may, by rule or order, prevent an adviser from taking custody. If an Administrator prevents custody, an adviser cannot overrule the Administrator by notifying the Administrator first.

3. **F.** An adviser may sell securities to clients from its own account provided disclosure is made upon receipt of written consent from the client prior to executing the trade.

4. **T.** Investment advisers are bound by the regulations that apply to sales activities as well as those that apply to advisory activities. The reverse is also true. When a sales agent engages in investment advisory activities, the agent is bound by the rules that apply to providing investment advice to others as well as those that apply to sales practices.

Unethical Business Practices HotSheet

Practices Prohibited of All Securities Professionals:

- Misleading or untrue statements
- Failure to state material facts
- Use of insider information
- Unsuitable transactions
- Market manipulation (pegging, front running, wash sales, matched purchases)

Other Prohibited Sales Practices:

- Unauthorized third-party trading
- Borrowing money from customers who are not banks, broker/dealers, or lending institutions
- Commingling client funds with those of the agent or the firm
- Failing to follow client instructions
- Exercising discretion without written authority
- Effecting transactions not on the books (selling away)
- Failing to report written complaints
- Guaranteeing against loss
- Failing to inform clients of higher than normal charges
- Misrepresenting customer account status
- Creating misleading trading activity
- Promising undeliverable services
- Unauthorized sharing in customer accounts
- Solicitation of unregistered, nonexempt securities
- Misrepresenting Administrator approval

Unlawful or Unethical Investment Advisory Practices:

- Unsuitable investments
- Unauthorized discretion
- Unauthorized third-party transactions
- Excessive trading
- Commingling funds
- Misrepresentation of material facts
- Nondisclosure of information sources
- Excessive fees
- Conflicts of interest
- Unauthorized custody of customer funds
- Operating without advisory contracts
- Performance-based compensation, when legally permitted
- Failing to disclose material legal action in past 10 years at least 48 hours before contracting with client
- Failing to disclose principal or agent capacity

Series 63
Unit Test 3

1. <u>Market manipulation</u> is one of the prohibited practices under the Uniform Securities
   Act. Which of the following is an example of
   a broker/dealer engaging in market
   manipulation?

   I. Churning
   II. Arbitrage·
   III. Front-running
   IV. Matched trades

   A. I and II only
   B. I, III and IV only
   C. III and IV only
   D. IV only

2. Your customer calls to check on her account
   value at 9:00 am You were unavailable at the
   time. It is now 2:00 p.m. and you are able to
   call her back. Between 9:00 am and 2:00 pm
   her account value dropped from $11,500 to
   $10,000. What should you say
   to her?

   A. "At the time that you called, your
      account had a value of $11,500."
   B. "Your account value cannot be deter-
      mined until the market closes."
   C. "Your account is valued at $10,000 at
      this time."
   D. "Your account was down to $9,700 ear-
      lier today but is up to $10,000."

3. All of the following are prohibited practices
   under the USA EXCEPT

   I. borrowing money or securities from the
      account of a former banker with express
      written permission
   II. failing to identify a customer's financial
       objectives ·
   III. selling rights
   IV. supplying funds to a client's account
       only when or if it declines below a pre-
       agreed-upon level

   A. I and II only
   B. I, II and III only
   C. II and IV only
   D. III only

4. A customer is upset with her agent for not
   servicing her account properly and sends
   him a complaint letter about his actions.
   Under the Uniform Securities Act, the agent
   should

   A. call the customer, apologize, and
      attempt to correct the problem
   B. tell the customer he is willing to make
      rescission
   C. do nothing
   D. bring the customer complaint to his
      employer immediately

5. Under the USA, the Administrator may
   deny or revoke a registration if an agent

   I. borrows money from his wealthy cli-
      ents' accounts
   II. solicits orders for non-exempt unregis-
       tered securities.
   III. buys and sells securities in accounts in
        order to generate a high level of
        commissions
   IV. alters market quotations in order to
       induce a client to invest in an attractive
       growth stock

   A. I and III only
   B. I and IV only
   C. I, II and III only
   D. I, II, III and IV

6. Under the Uniform Securities Act, an investment adviser may legally have custody of money or securities belonging to a client if the

   I. adviser is not bonded
   II. Administrator has not prohibited custodial arrangements
   III. adviser does not also have discretionary authority over the account
   IV. adviser has notified the Administrator that he has custody

   A. I and III only
   B. II only
   C. II and IV only
   D. IV only

7. According to the USA, which of the following is an example of market manipulation?

   A. Creating the illusion of active trading
   B. Omitting material facts in a presentation
   C. Guaranteeing performance of a security
   D. Transactions in excess of a customer's financial capability

8. A federal covered investment adviser is one who

   I. has $30 million or more under management
   II. manages an investment company registered under the Investment Company Act of 1940
   III. limits his advice to securities listed on the NYSE
   IV. is affiliated with a federally chartered bank

   A. I and II only
   B. I and III only
   C. II and III only
   D. I, II, III and IV

9. Which of the following practices is prohibited under the USA?

   A. Participating in active trading of a security in which an unusually high trading volume has occurred
   B. Offering services that an agent cannot realistically perform because of his broker/dealer's limitations
   C. Altering the customer's order at the request of a customer which subsequently results in a substantial loss
   D. Failing to inform the firm's principal of frequent oral customer complaints

10. An agent hears a rumor concerning a security and uses the rumor to convince a client to purchase the security. Under the USA, the agent may

    A. recommend the security if it is an appropriate investment
    B. recommend the investment if the rumor is based on material inside information
    C. recommend the security if the source of the rumor came from a reliable source
    D. not recommend the security

11. If an agent thinks that a technology stock is undervalued and actively solicits all customers, the agent

    I. did not violate the USA if all material facts are disclosed
    II. committed an unethical sales practice because the firm has not recommended this technology stock
    III. committed an unethical business practice
    IV. did not commit a violation if all clients are accurately informed of the price of the stock

    A. I, II and IV only
    B. I and IV only
    C. III only
    D. I, II, III and IV

12. Which of the following transactions are prohibited?

    I. Borrowing money or securities from a high net-worth customer

    II. Selling speculative or hot issues to a retired couple of modest means on a fixed income

    III. Failing to follow a customer's orders so as to prevent investment in a security not adequately covered by well-known securities analysts

    IV. Backdating confirmations for the benefit of the client's tax reporting

    A. I and II only
    B. II and III only
    C. I, II and III only
    D. I, II, III and IV

13. It is legal under the USA for a registered investment adviser to tell a client that

    A. a registered security may lawfully be sold in that state.
    B. an exempt security is not required to be registered because it is generally regarded as being safer than a nonexempt security
    C. her qualifications have been found satisfactory by the Administrator
    D. a registered security has been approved for sale in the state by the Administrator

14. An agent omits facts that a prudent investor requires in order to make informed decisions. Under the Uniform Securities Act, this action is

    A. fraudulent for nonexempt securities only
    B. fraudulent for exempt securities only
    C. fraudulent for both exempt and nonexempt securities
    D. not fraudulent if there was willful intent to omit the information

15. Which of the following actions is not a prohibited practice under the USA?

    A. A market maker fills his firm's order ahead of a customer order at the same price.
    B. A specialist buys and sells stock as principal.
    C. A principal of a broker/dealer allows a rumor to leak out that ABC is going to acquire LMN; after a few days, the broker/dealer sells ABC short for its own account.
    D. An agent sells a customer's stock at the bid price and makes up the difference with a personal check.

16. Which of the following is(are) prohibited under the USA?

    I. Recommending tax shelters to low income retirees

    II. Stating that a state Administrator has approved an offering based on the quality of information found in the prospectus

    III. Soliciting orders for unregistered, nonexempt securities

    IV. Employing any device to defraud

    A. I only
    B. I and II only
    C. I, II and III only
    D. I, II, III and IV

17. According to the Uniform Securities Act, an investment adviser may have custody of a customer's funds and securities if

    A. it has received the permission of the Administrator
    B. it has received permission from the SEC
    C. it does not share in the capital gains of the account
    D. the Administrator has been informed of the custody

18. According to the USA, which of the following is a prohibited activity?

   A. The agent enters into an agreement to share in the profits/losses of the customer's account without an investment in the account.
   B. The agent and his spouse jointly own their own personal trading account at the firm.
   C. The agent, with his firm's and the client's permission, participates in the profits and losses of the account in proportion to his investment in the account.
   D. An agent refuses a client's request to share in the performance of the client's account.

19. A registered broker/dealer is under common control with a registered investment adviser. An individual who is an agent of the broker/dealer and an investment adviser representative of the adviser has a client with $250,000 under an asset management program. This individual calls the client and suggests the purchase of 500 shares of RMBM common stock as an appropriate addition to the portfolio. The broker/dealer is a market maker in RMBM and the sale will be made as a principal, a fact that is disclosed to the client on the trade confirmation. In this situation, the registered person has acted

   A. lawfully in that the disclosure of capacity was made on the confirmation
   B. lawfully in that disclosure of capacity is not necessary when executing trades in managed accounts
   C. unlawfully in that any stock the broker/dealer is a market maker in is probably not suitable for a managed money client
   D. unlawfully in that investment advisers are required to make written disclosure in advance of a trade where the firm or an affiliate will be acting in a principal capacity and receive the client's consent

20. Which of the following are prohibited practices?

   I. An investment advisory firm organized as a partnership failed to inform its clients of the departure of a partner with a very small interest in the partnership
   II. An investment advisory firm charges an annual fee equal to 2% of the first $250,000 in assets under management; 1% of the next $500,000 and .5% for everything in excess of $750,000
   III. The majority stockholder of a registered investment adviser pledges his stock as collateral for a loan taken out by the firm to expand its services without obtaining client consent for assignment of their contracts
   IV. Engaging in agency cross transactions

   A. I, II, III and IV
   B. I, and III only
   C. I and IV only
   D. III and IV only

Series 63 Unit Test 3 Answers & Rationale

1.   C.   Front-running, the practice of entering an order for the benefit of the firm ahead of a customer order, is a form of market manipulation. Matched trades or matched purchases occur when market participants agree to buy and sell securities among themselves in order to create the appearance of heightened market activity; this is also a form of market manipulation. While churning is a prohibited practice, it does not involve manipulating the market, and arbitrage is the perfectly legal practice of buying a security in one marketplace and simultaneously selling it in another to benefit from a price discrepancy.

2.   C.   All other choices are clearly a misrepresentation of account status.

3.   D.   It is permissible to sell rights, which are securities. Borrowing money or securities from other than a bank or broker/dealer in the business of lending, failing to identify a customer's financial objectives, and guaranteeing a customer's account against losses are all prohibited practices.

4.   D.   Failure to bring customers' written complaints to the attention of the agent's broker/dealer is prohibited.

5.   D.   An Administrator may deny or revoke an agent's registration if the agent engages in prohibited practices such as those described in each of the choices in the question.

6.   C.   The Administrator may prohibit advisers from having custody of client funds or securities. If no such prohibition applies, the Administrator must be notified in writing if an adviser has custody. In almost all jurisdictions, a bond or sufficient net worth is required to maintain custody. Discretionary authority does not affect an adviser's ability to have custody.

7.   A.   Creating the illusion of trading activity is market manipulation. Guaranteeing performance of a security and omitting material facts are prohibited practices but do not constitute market manipulation. Trades too large for a customer are also prohibited because they are not suitable.

8.   A.   Federal registration is required of any investment adviser managing at least $30 million in assets. It is optional at $25 million; anything less requires state registration. NSMIA provides that any investment adviser under contract to a registered investment company under the Investment Company Act of 1940 is required to register with the SEC as a federal covered adviser. Providing advice on federal covered securities listed on the NYSE does not make the advisor a federal covered adviser. Banks and their representatives are always excluded from the definition of an investment adviser, federal covered or not.

9.   B.   An agent may not offer services that he cannot perform. Choice A is incorrect because an agent may participate actively in trading a security in which an unusually high trading volume has occurred, provided the trading is not designed to create a false appearance of high volume. C is incorrect because an agent can alter a client's order, even if the change results in a loss. D is incorrect because an agent is only required to report written complaints to his employing principal, although it would be wise to report repeated complaints if they are serious.

10.   D.   The use of information, such as a rumor, that has no basis in fact is prohibited. The key here is that the agent recommended this stock to all clients.

11.   C.   Agents must always determine suitability before soliciting purchases or sales. An investment cannot be suitable for all of your clients.

12. D. All of the practices are prohibited. An agent may not borrow money or securities from a customer unless that customer is a bank or broker/dealer in the business of lending money and/or securities. Selling speculative or hot issues to a retired couple of modest means is an unsuitable transaction because it is not consistent with the objectives of the client. An agent must follow legal orders of the customer, even if the agent believes the order is an unwise one. An agent may not backdate confirmations for the benefit of the client.

13. A. An agent may indicate that a security is registered or is exempt from registration. All of the other statements are illegal.

14. C. Material facts are facts that an investor relies on to make investment decisions. The omission of a material fact in the sale, purchase, or offer of a security is fraudulent. This applies whether the security offered is exempt or nonexempt.

15. B. The function of the specialist is to act as a broker for orders left with him by other broker/dealers and to act as a dealer in buying and selling for his own account. His activity is not prohibited. Allowing a rumor to leak out and then trade on it is a prohibited practice. Selling stock at the bid price and making up the difference with a personal check is a prohibited practice. Filling a firm's proprietary order ahead of a customer's order is a prohibited practice called front-running.

16. D. All of the choices are prohibited. Recommending tax shelters to low income retirees is an example of an unsuitable transaction. Stating that an Administrator has approved an offering based on the quality of information in the prospectus, soliciting orders for unregistered nonexempt securities, and employing a device to defraud are all prohibited practices under the USA.

17. D. As long as retaining custody of funds is not prohibited, an investment adviser may have custody of a customer's account after providing notice to the Administrator.

18. A. Under the USA, it is a prohibited practice under the USA for an agent to share in the profits or losses of a customer's account unless the customer and the employer have given written consent and the percentage of participation is proportionate to the percentage of the agent's personal funds in the account. An agent is permitted to jointly own a personal account at the firm, and can refuse to share in a customer's account.

19. D. The rules regarding investment advisers and account trading are much stricter than those for broker/dealers due to the fiduciary responsibility of the adviser. Any action that results in a transaction in which the firm or an affiliate acts in either a principal or agency capacity requires prior written disclosure of that fact to the client and approval of the client.

20. B. Any change in the ownership of an investment advisory firm organized as a partnership, no matter how small, requires notification to all clients within a reasonable amount of time. If the firm is structured as a corporation, the pledging of a controlling interest in the company's stock is viewed as an assignment of the contracts. This may not be done without the approval of the clients. The fee structure proposed in Choice II is fine. Agency cross transactions, that is, where the adviser represents both sides of the trade, are permitted as long as the adviser makes the proper written disclosures and does not make the buy/sell recommendations to either party.

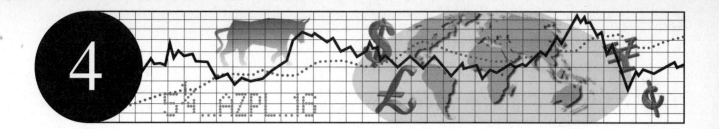

4

The Administrative Provisions of the Uniform Securities Act

INTRODUCTION

This unit discusses the origins of the **Uniform Securities Act** (USA) and addresses the jurisdiction and the powers of the **Administrator**, the person in charge of enforcing the law in each state.

The USA is model legislation that arose in an effort to unify numerous state securities laws, known as **blue-sky laws**. Under the USA, the state Administrator has jurisdiction over securities transactions that originate in, are directed into, or are accepted in the Administrator's state. For those persons or transactions that fall within the jurisdiction of the Administrator, the Administrator has power to: make rules and orders; conduct investigations and issue subpoenas; issue cease and desist orders; and deny, suspend, or revoke registrations.

The USA provides both civil liabilities and criminal penalties for violating the act. Civil liabilities enable an investor to recover attorney's fees and losses resulting from securities sold in violation of the USA. Criminal penalties in addition to the civil liabilities may be levied against those who engage in fraudulent activities under the act.

The Series 63 exam will include approximately 6 questions on the material presented in this unit.

UNIT OBJECTIVES

When you have completed this unit, you should be able to:

- understand the relationship between state and national securities laws;
- recognize the jurisdiction of the state securities Administrator;
- list the powers of the Administrator within its jurisdiction;
- describe the rights of recovery for a security's sale or for investment advice purchased in violation of the USA; and
- contrast civil and criminal penalties for violation of the act.

Origins of the Uniform Securities Act

Financial markets developed along with the industrialization of the United States. As a result of new commercial opportunities, corporations issued securities to the public to fund their growth and development. Each state enacted securities laws to regulate the sale of these securities within their states.

The first state to enact a securities law, known as a **blue-sky law**, was Kansas in 1911. The term *blue-sky* was coined by a Kansas Supreme Court justice who considered some of these newly issued securities as nothing more than "speculative schemes that have no more basis than so many feet of blue sky."

After the adoption of the first act, the idea of securities regulation began to spread and by 1913, twenty-three other jurisdictions had adopted securities acts. By the time of the Great Depression in 1929, virtually all of the states had some form of securities act. The stock market crash of 1929 precipitated a movement to create a federal securities agency that could deal with schemes involving interstate commerce. This movement culminated in the passage of the Securities Act of 1933 and the Securities Exchange Act of 1934. Thus, state securities regulation predated federal securities regulation by some 20 years.

USA as Model State Legislation

With the enactment of national securities legislation (e.g., the Securities Act of 1933 and the Securities and Exchange Act of 1934) and numerous states blue-sky laws, the need for uniformity in securities laws among the states arose. In 1956, the **National Conference of Commissioners on Uniform State Laws (NCCUSL)**, a national organization of lawyers devoted to unifying state laws, drafted the original Uniform Securities Act.

The **Uniform Securities Act (USA)** is model (ideal) legislation, not actual legislation. In other words, the USA is a template or guide that each state uses in drafting its securities legislation. The securities laws of most states follow the USA very closely, and in many cases, almost exactly.

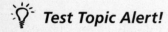 **Test Topic Alert!**

The Series 63 exam tests your knowledge of the USA, not the specifics of your state's securities legislation. The USA is periodically updated to adjust to developments in the securities markets. You will be tested on the latest version of the USA, endorsed by the North American Securities Administrators Association (NASAA), the advisory body of state securities regulators.

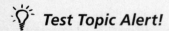 **Test Topic Alert!**

The Series 63 is a "law" exam and therefore unlike other securities exams. NASAA requires that you not only know what the law says, but that you also are able to apply the law to concrete examples—general knowledge of the law is not enough. On the test you will be asked to apply the law to situations that may arise in the business.

USA Reflects The National Securities Markets Improvement Act of 1996 and Securities Litigation Uniform Standards Act of 1998

While the USA was drafted by the NCCUSL to unify the blue-sky laws among the states, the **National Securities Markets Improvement Act of 1996 (NSMIA)** was enacted by Congress to eliminate conflicts between federal and state laws. In an effort to increase market efficiency, NSMIA gave the SEC the duty to eliminate overlapping (or dual) state and federal securities regulation. Under NSMIA, securities regulatory responsibilities are divided between federal and state governments. Those securities and transactions regulated by federal law are referred to as **federal covered securities** or **federal covered transactions**.

The **Securities Litigation Uniform Standards Act of 1998 (SLUSA)** allows federal courts to preempt state courts in class action fraud cases. The act ensures that state securities class actions will be governed by the uniform standards of federal law.

Federal Covered Securities and Transactions

NSMIA prohibits states from regulating public offerings; proxy solicitations; and the required disclosures of securities that trade on the New York Stock Exchange and the American Stock Exchange, or are Nasdaq National Market securities. NSMIA also prohibits states from requiring state registration of securities regulated by a national regulatory body such as the SEC. These securities and transactions are **covered** (**regulated**) by federal laws (e.g., the Securities Act of 1933 and the Investment Company Act of 1940) and cannot be regulated by the state law.

✓ **For Example:** A security traded on the New York Stock Exchange (e.g., IBM) is a federal covered security. Therefore, it must register its securities with the SEC. Under NSMIA, a state could not also require IBM to register its securities with the state because its securities are covered by federal legislation (in this case, the Securities Act of 1933).

Additional examples of federal covered securities are securities:

- issued by an open-end investment company (a mutual fund), closed-end investment company, unit investment trust, or face amount certificate company that is registered under the Investment Company Act of 1940;
- offered by a municipal/governmental issuer, unless the issuer is located in the state in which the securities are being offered; or
- offered by an issuer exclusively to its existing security holders where no commissions or other remuneration is paid directly or indirectly for soliciting the exchange.

The Administrator of the Uniform Securities Act

Administrator   The state official charged with enforcement of the USA in the state is called the **Administrator**. The Administrator can be an individual (such as a securities commissioner) or a division within a larger state agency (such as the office of the Secretary of State).

✓ ***Take Note:*** Like most securities legislation, the USA is designed to prevent fraud in the sale of securities to the general public. To guard against fraud, the USA grants the Administrator broad powers over the issuance of securities and registration of individuals who deal in those securities within the Administrator's state.

 Quick Quiz 4.1

1. Which of the following statements are TRUE?

   I. The Uniform Securities Act is not the actual law of any state or territory of the United States.
   II. The National Securities Markets Improvement Act of 1996 requires states and the federal government to have identical registration requirements.
   III. The state securities Administrator has responsibility for the enforcement and administration of a state's securities law.

   A. I and II only
   B. I and III only
   C. II and III only
   D. I, II and III

2. The term *federal covered security* would include all of the following EXCEPT

   A. XYZ common stock, listed on the American Stock Exchange
   B. ABC growth fund, a mutual fund registered as an investment company under the Investment Company Act of 1940
   C. GHIJ common stock, a biotech concern traded on the Nasdaq SmallCap market
   D. Treasury Notes

Answers

1. **B.** *The Uniform Securities Act is not the actual law of any state or territory. Rather, it is model legislation that states use as a guide in drafting their own securities laws. Those laws give the responsibility to the state Administrator for enforcement and administration of those laws. NSMIA's purpose is to eliminate dual registration and registration, not to require identical laws.*

2. **C.** *The only Nasdaq traded securities that qualify for the designation as federal covered securities are those on the national market system, not the SmallCap. Stocks listed on the NYSE, investment companies registered under the*

Investment Company Act of 1940, and securities issued by the US government fall within the definition.

Jurisdiction and Powers of the State Administrator

The jurisdiction and powers of the Administrator extend to activities related to the sale of securities.

Terminology

Sale or Sell The USA defines the term **sale** or **sell** to include every contract of sale, contract to sell, and disposition of a security or interest in a security for value.

✓ **Take Note:** Any transfer of a security in which money or some other valuable consideration is involved is covered by this definition and subject to the act.

Offer or Offer to Sell The USA defines the terms **offer** or **offer to sell** to include every attempt or offer to dispose of, or solicitation of an offer to buy a security or interest in a security for value. These terms include any:

- security given or delivered with, or as a bonus on account of, any purchase of securities or other items constituting part of the purchase;
- gift of assessable stock (assessable stock is stock issued below par for which the issuer or creditors have the right to assess shareholders for the balance of unpaid par); or
- warrant or right to purchase or subscribe to another security (an offer of the other security is considered to be included in the warrant or right).

✓ **For Example:** If a car dealer, as an essential part of a sale, offers $1,000 in corporate bonds as an incentive, this would be considered a bonus under the act and, therefore, this sale falls under the jurisdiction of the state securities Administrator.

✓ **Take Note:** When assessable stock is given as a gift, the Administrator has jurisdiction over the transaction because there is a potential future obligation in that either the issuer, or more likely, creditors can demand payment for the balance of the par value.

✓ **For Example:** If an individual owned assessable stock and felt that the issuer was on the verge of bankruptcy, that person could give the stock as a "present." If the bankruptcy occurred, the new owner would then be subject to the assessment.

Test Topic Alert! There is no longer any assessable stock in existence, but the exam may ask about it anyway.

The terms *offer* or *offer to sell* do not include any:

- bona fide pledge or loan;
- gift of non-assessable stock;
- stock dividend, if nothing of value is given by the stockholders for the dividend;
- class vote by stockholders, pursuant to the certificate of incorporation or the applicable corporation statute, on a merger, consolidation, reclassification of securities, or sale of corporate assets in consideration of the issuance of securities of another corporation; or
- act incident to a judicially approved reorganization with which a security is issued in exchange for one or more outstanding securities, claims, or property interest, or partly in such exchange and partly for cash.

Jurisdiction of the Administrator

Under law, for any agent of a state (e.g., the Administrator) to have authority over an activity such as a sale or offer of securities, it must have **legal jurisdiction to act.** Jurisdiction under the USA specifically means the **legal authority** to regulate securities activities that take place in the state.

The USA describes those activities considered to have taken place in the state. They are defined as any offer to buy or sell a security, as well as any acceptance of the offer, if the offer:

- **originated in** the Administrator's state;
- is **directed to** the Administrator's state; or
- is **accepted in** the Administrator's state.

✔ *Take Note:* Since securities transactions often involve several states, more than one Administrator may have jurisdiction over a security or a transaction.

☀ *Case Study: Offer Originated in Administrator's State*

Situation: Mr. Thompson (a registered agent in Illinois), on the recommendation of his best client (Mr. Bixby), phones a friend of Mr. Bixby's in Indiana. Mr. Thompson sells a security to Mr. Bixby's friend, Ms. Gordon, who then mails payment to Mr. Thompson's office in Illinois.

Analysis: The Administrators of both Illinois and Indiana have jurisdiction— the Administrator of Illinois has jurisdiction because the call (offer) originated in Illinois and the Administrator of Indiana has jurisdiction because the offer was *accepted* by Ms. Gordon in Indiana.

☀ *Case Study: Offer Directed to Administrator's State*

Situation: On the day after he completed his first transaction with Ms. Gordon, Mr. Thompson mails sales offering materials to her home address in Indiana. Ms. Gordon is not in a position to buy any more securities, so she discards the material without reading it.

Analysis: By sending sales materials to Ms. Gordon's home address in Indiana, Mr. Thompson directed the offer to Indiana. Even though Ms. Gordon discarded the information, the Administrator in Indiana has jurisdiction because the sales offer was directed to Indiana. The Administrator of Illinois also has jurisdiction because the offer originated in Illinois.

Case Study: Offer Accepted in an Administrator's State

Situation: Mr. Thompson sends additional offers to Ms. Gordon in Indiana who is now on a three-month summer vacation in Florida. Ms. Gordon has her mail forwarded to her in Florida. Upon receiving Mr. Thompson's materials in Florida, she decides to purchase the securities. She pays for the securities by mailing a check to Mr. Thompson drawn on her local bank in Indiana.

Analysis: The offer is accepted by Ms. Gordon while she was in Florida and, therefore, the Administrator of Florida has jurisdiction. Additionally, the Administrator in Illinois has jurisdiction because the offer originated in Illinois and the Administrator in Indiana has jurisdiction because the offer was directed to Indiana. This is a situation where the Administrators of three different states have jurisdiction.

Publishing and Broadcast Exceptions to Jurisdiction

There are special rules regarding the Administrator's jurisdiction over offers made through a TV or radio broadcast or through a bona fide newspaper.

The USA specifies that an offer would not be made in an Administrator's state and, therefore, the Administrator would not have jurisdiction if it were made under any of the following circumstances:

- television or radio broadcast that originated outside of the state;
- bona fide newspaper or periodical published outside of the state; or
- newspaper or periodical published inside the state but has more than two-thirds (66%) of its circulation outside the state in the last year.

✓ **Take Note:** A bona fide newspaper is a newspaper of general interest and circulation, such as *The New York Times*. Private investment advisory newsletters, usually distributed by subscription, are not bona fide newspapers and therefore do not fall under the publishing exception.

Case Study: Publishing and Broadcast Exemptions

Situation: First Securities & Co., broker/dealers with offices in New York State and Illinois, offers to sell shares in a new retail shoe chain store located in New York. First Securities advertises the offering to residents of New York in the local newspaper, the *New York Gazette*. First Securities also advertises through the *Gazette's* wholly owned radio station. The *Gazette* and its radio station are both located in western New York near the Pennsylvania border. About 55% of the *Gazette's* readers and listeners live in Pennsylvania.

Analysis: Although more than half the readers and listeners of the *Gazette* live in Pennsylvania, under the terms of the publishing and broadcasting exemption of the USA, the offer is *not* made in Pennsylvania since the paper is not published in Pennsylvania, so the Administrator of New York State has sole jurisdiction over the offering. No dual or multiple jurisdictions applies in this case unless the offer is actually accepted in Pennsylvania. The fact that

First Securities is registered in Illinois in addition to New York is not relevant to this offering because no securities were sold there, nor were any offers or advertising directed to the state.

Quick Quiz 4.2

1. A state's securities Administrator has jurisdiction over a securities offering if it was

   A. directed to residents of that state
   B. originated in that state
   C. accepted in that state
   D. all of the above

2. An Administrator has jurisdiction over an offer to sell securities if it is made in a newspaper published within the state with no more than

   A. one-third of its circulation outside the state
   B. one-half of its circulation outside the state
   C. two-thirds of its circulation outside the state
   D. 90% of its circulation outside the state

Answers

1. **D**. *The Administrator has jurisdiction over a security offering if it was directed to, originated in, or was accepted in that state.*

2. **C**. *A state Administrator has jurisdiction over a securities offering made in a bona fide newspaper published within the state, but only whose circulation is less than two-thirds outside the state.*

Powers of the Administrator

The USA not only establishes the jurisdiction of the Administrator but also outlines the powers that the Administrator has within that jurisdiction. The USA provides the Administrator with four broad powers with which to enforce and administer the act.

The Administrator has the power or authority to:

- make, amend, or rescind rules and orders;
- conduct investigations and issue subpoenas;
- issue cease and desist orders and seek injunctions; and
- deny, suspend, cancel, or revoke registrations and licenses.

While the Administrator and his employees have powers to enforce the act for the benefit of the public, the Administrator also has the obligation not to misuse the office for personal gain.

For Example: The Administrator, the officers, and the employees are prohibited from using, for their own benefit, any information derived from their official responsibilities that has not been made public.

Make, Amend, or Rescind Rules and Orders

To enforce the USA, the Administrator has authority to **make**, **amend**, or **rescind rules** and orders necessary to administer the act. The Administrator may also issue interpretive letters. The USA requires that all rules and orders be published. A rule or order of the Administrator has the same authority as a provision of the act itself but these rules and orders are not part of the USA itself. The difference between a rule and an order is that a **rule** applies to everyone while an **order** applies to a specific instance.

 For Example: The Administrator may decide to issue a ruling requiring all agents to pay an annual registration fee of $250. That applies to everyone. Or, the Administrator may find that a specific agent has violated a provision of the law and orders a 30-day suspension. That order applies only to that particular agent.

An individual may challenge an order of the Administrator in court within 60 days of order issuance.

While the Administrator has the power to make and amend rules for compliance with state blue-sky law, he does not have the power to alter the law itself.

The composition or content of state securities law is the responsibility of the state legislature and not that of administrative agencies. Rules for administration and compliance with the law are the responsibility of the securities Administrator.

Case Study: Rules and Orders of the Administrator

Situation: The Iowa state securities Administrator requires by rule that all companies registering their securities in Iowa must supply financial statements in a specific form and with content prescribed by the Administrator. However, the Administrator does not publish the rule because the rule is too long and complex.

Analysis: The USA allows state Administrators to issue rules and orders in carrying out their regulatory functions and the Iowa Administrator acted quite properly in designing the form and content for financial reports. However, it is required by the USA that Administrators publish all rules and orders. The Administrator, despite the latitude given it in administering the USA, cannot suspend any provision of the USA itself. The Iowa Administrator acted within its authority in designing the forms but acted without authority—that is, he violated the USA—by suspending the requirement that all rules and orders be published.

Conduct Investigations and Issue Subpoenas

The Administrator has broad discretionary authority to **conduct investigations** and **issue subpoenas**. These investigations may be made in public or in private and may occur within or outside of the Administrator's state.

These investigations are normally open to the public, but when in the opinion of the Administrator, and with the consent of all parties, it is felt that a private investigation is more appropriate, that investigation will be conducted without public scrutiny.

In conducting an investigation, the Administrator has the power to:

- require statements in writing, under oath, as to all matters relating to the issue under investigation;
- publish and make public the facts and circumstances concerning the issue to be investigated;
- subpoena witnesses and compel their attendance and testimony; and
- take evidence and require the production of books, papers, correspondence, and any other documents deemed relevant.

✓ *Take Note:* In addition to the power to conduct investigations, the Administrator may enforce subpoenas issued by Administrators in other states on the same basis as if the alleged offense took place in the Administrator's state.

Issue Cease and Desist Orders

If an Administrator determines that a person is about to engage in an activity that constitutes a violation of the USA, the Administrator may issue a **cease and desist order** without a hearing. The Administrator is granted this power to prevent potential violations before they occur.

Although the Administrator has the power to issue cease and desist orders, it does not have the legal power to compel compliance with the order. To compel compliance in the face of an individual's resistance, the Administrator must apply to a court of competent jurisdiction for an **injunction**. Only the courts can compel compliance by issuing injunctions and imposing penalties for violation of them.

✓ *Take Note:* Cease and desist orders are not the same as stop orders. Cease and desist orders are directed at individuals requiring them to cease activities. Stop orders are directed to registration applications.

☼ Case Study: Cease and Desist Orders

Situation: Mr. Thompson is properly registered to conduct business in the state of Illinois and makes plans to sell a security within the next few days. The Administrator considers this security ineligible for sale in the state. The Administrator orders Thompson to immediately stop his sales procedures.

Analysis: The Administrator of Illinois issued a cease and desist order to Thompson because there was not sufficient time to conduct a public hearing prior to the sale to determine if the security was eligible for sale in the state.

Deny, Suspend, Cancel, or Revoke Registrations

The Administrator has the power to deny, suspend, cancel, or revoke the registration of broker/dealers, investment advisers, and their representatives, as well as those of securities issues.

Broker/Dealers, Advisers, and their Representatives

To justify a denial, revocation, or suspension of the license of a **securities professional**, the Administrator must find that the order is in the public interest and also find that the individual:

- has filed an incomplete, false, or misleading registration application;
- willfully violated the Uniform Securities Act;
- has been convicted of a securities-related misdemeanor within the last 10 years;
- has been convicted of any felony within the last 10 years;
- has been enjoined by law from engaging in the securities business;
- is subject to an Administrator's denial, revocation, or suspension;
- is engaged in dishonest or unethical securities practices;
- is insolvent;
- has failed to pay application filing fees; or
- is not qualified on the basis of training, lack of experience, and knowledge of the securities business.

✓ **Take Note:** The public's best interest is not reason enough for the denial, suspension, or revocation of a registration. There must be a further reason, such as described above.

The Administrator must notify the registrant of any reason to deny, suspend, revoke, or cancel a registration, and if asked in writing, must provide a hearing within 15 days. The Administrator may not stop a registration on the basis of facts that were known to the Administrator at the time the registration became effective (unless the proceedings are initiated within 30 days).

Securities Issues

As is the case with a securities professsonal, a securities Administrator may deny, suspend, cancel, or revoke a securities registration if the order is in the public's interest and the securities registrant:

- files a misleading or incomplete registration statement;
- is engaged in an offering that is fraudulent or made on unfair, unjust, or inequitable terms;
- charges offering fees that are excessive or unreasonable;
- is subject to a court injunction; or
- is engaged in a method of business that is illegal.

✓ **Take Note:** There are different reasons for stopping the registrations of persons and of issues. For instance, the Administrator can deny a registration if an underwriter charges offering fees that are excessive. No such provision applies to a securities professional registering for a license.

Quick Quiz 4.3

1. With regard to the powers of the Administrator, which of the following statements are FALSE?

   I. The Administrator must seek an injunction to issue a cease and desist order.
   II. The USA requires an Administrator to conduct a full hearing, public or private, prior to issuing a cease and desist order.
   III. The USA grants the Administrator the power to issue injunctions to force compliance with the provisions of the act.

   A. I and II only
   B. I and III only
   C. II and III only
   D. I, II and III

2. While the Administrator has great power, the USA does place some limitations on the office. Which of the following statements regarding those powers are TRUE?

   I. In conducting an investigation, an Administrator can compel the testimony of witnesses.
   II. Investigations of serious violations must be open to the public.
   III. An Administrator in Illinois may only enforce subpoenas from South Carolina if the violation originally occurred in Illinois.
   IV. An administrator may deny the registration of a securities professional who has been convicted of any felony within the past 10 years, but must provide, if requested in writing, a hearing within 15 days.

   A. I and IV only
   B. I, II and IV only
   C. II and III only
   D. I, III and IV only

Answers

1. **D.** *All of these are false statements. The Administrator need not seek an injunction to issue a cease and desist order. The USA does not require that an Administrator conduct a public or private hearing prior to issuing a cease and desist order. When time does not permit, the Administrator may issue a cease and desist prior to a hearing to prevent a pending violation. The USA does not grant the Administrator the power to issue injunctions to force compliance with the act. The act permits the Administrator to issue cease and desist orders and, if they do not work, the Administrator may seek an injunction from a court of competent jurisdiction. A cease and desist order is an administrative order whereas an injunction is a judicial order.*

2. **A.** *An Administrator can compel the testimony of witnesses when conducting an investigation. Investigation of serious violations need not be held in public. An Administrator in Illinois may enforce subpoenas from South Carolina whether the violation occurred in Illinois or not. Conviction for any felony within the past 10 years is one of a number of reasons that the Administrator has for denying*

*a license. However, upon notice of the denial, a written request may be made
for a hearing. That request must be honored within 15 days.*

Nonpunitive Terminations of Registration

A registration can be terminated even if there has not been a violation of the
Uniform Securities Act. A request for withdrawal and lack of qualification
are all reasons for cancellation.

Withdrawal

A person, on their own initiative, may request a **withdrawal** of a registration.
The withdrawal is effective 30 days after the Administrator receives it, provided no revocation or suspension proceedings are in process against the
person making the request.

Lack of Qualification

An Administrator may not base a denial of an individual's registration solely
on their **lack of experience**. However, the USA allows the Administrator to
restrict an applicant's registration for an investment adviser's license to that
of a sales agent or registered representative if that person is not qualified to
function as an investment adviser.

Cancellation

If an Administrator finds that an applicant or a registrant no longer exists or
has ceased to transact business, the Administrator may **cancel** the
registration.

 Test Topic Alert!

You may encounter this type of question regarding cancellation: "What would
the Administrator do if mailings to a registrant are returned with no forward-
ing address?" The answer choice is "The registration is cancelled."

The Administrator may also cancel a registration if a person is declared mentally incompetent.

✓ **Take Note:** Be familiar with the distinctions between cancellation and
denial, suspension, or revocation. Cancellation does not result from violations
or a failure to follow the provisions of the act. Cancellation occurs as the result
of death, dissolution, or mental incompetency.

 **Quick Quiz 4.4**

1. All of the following statements relating to termination of registration are <u>false</u> EXCEPT

   A. A registration, once in effect, may never be <u>voluntarily</u> withdrawn. *F*

   B. An Adminitrator may not cancel a registration of a securities professional who is declared <u>mentally incompetent.</u> *F*

   C. An Administrator may revoke the registration of a securities professional who is declared mentally incompetent. *Cancel* *F*

   D. An administrator may cancel the registration of a registrant no longer in business. *T*

Answers

1. **D.** *An administrator may cancel the registration of a registrant that is no longer in existence. A person may request a withdrawal of a registration. Withdrawals become effective after 30 days if there are no revocation or denial proceedings in process. An Administrator does not revoke the registration of a person who is declared mentally incompetent but cancels such registration; this is a non-punitive administrative action.*

Penalties for Violations of the Uniform Securities Act

The USA provides both **civil liabilities** and **criminal penalties** for persons who violate the USA. In addition, the act provides for <u>recovery by a client of financial loss that results from the fraudulent sale of a security or investment advice</u>.

Civil Liabilities

Persons who sell securities or who offer investment advice in violation of the USA are subject to **civil liabilities** (as well as criminal penalties). <u>Enforcement of civil liabilities under the USA is subject to the **Securities Litigation Uniform Standards Act of 1998**</u>.

The purchaser of securities sold in violation of the act may sue the seller to recover financial loss.

The purchaser can sue for recovery if the:

- securities were sold in violation of the registration provisions of USA;
- securities professional <u>omits</u> or <u>makes an untrue statement</u> of material fact;
- securities were sold by an agent who should have been but was not <u>registered under the act</u>; or

- securities were sold in violation of a rule or order of the securities Administrator.

Statute of Limitations

The time limits, or statute of limitations, for violations of the civil provisions of the Uniform Securities Act is three years from the date of sale (rendering of the investment advice), or two years after discovering the violation, whichever comes first.

Rights of Recovery from Improper Sale of Securities

If the seller of securities discovers that they have made a sale in violation of the USA, the seller may offer to repurchase the securities from the buyer. In this case, the seller is offering the buyer the **right of rescission**. To satisfy the buyer's right to rescission, the amount paid back to the buyer must include the original purchase price and interest as determined by the Administrator.

By offering to buy back the securities that were sold in violation of the act, the seller can avoid a lawsuit through a **letter of rescission**. The buyer has 30 days after receiving the letter of rescission to respond. If the buyer does not accept the rescission offer within 30 days, the buyer gives up any right to pursue a lawsuit at a later date.

If the buyer accepts the rescission offer, he may recover:

- the original purchase price of the securities; *plus*
- any interest costs as determined by the Administrator; *plus*
- all reasonable attorney's fees; *minus*
- any income received during the period that the securities were held.

Rights of Recovery from Improper Investment Advice

A person who buys a security as the result of investment advice received in violation of the USA also has the right of rescission. In the case of securities purchased as a result of improper investment advice, the buyer may recover:

- cost of the advice; *plus*
- loss as a result of the advice; *plus*
- all interest costs from date of fee payment as determined by the Administrator; *plus*
- any reasonable attorney's fees.

✓ **Take Note:** When securities are sold improperly, the buyer can recover the original purchase price in addition to other losses. When improper investment advice is offered, the purchaser of the advice is entitled to recover the cost of the advice and losses incurred, but is not entitled to recover the original purchase price from the adviser.

Criminal Penalties

Persons found guilty of a fraudulent securities transaction are subject to **criminal penalties** (as well as civil liabilities). Upon conviction, a person may be fined or imprisoned, or both. To be convicted of **fraud**, the violation must be willful and the registrant must know that the activity is fraudulent.

✓ ***Take Note:*** **Fraud** is the deliberate or willful concealment, misrepresentation, or omission of material information or the truth in order to deceive or manipulate another person for unlawful or unfair gain.

Statute of Limitations

The statute of limitations for criminal offenses under the USA is five years from the date of the offense.

✓ ***Take Note:*** Remember the sequence of 5-5-3 for the application of *criminal* penalties; 5-year statute of limitations, $5,000 maximum fine, and imprisonment of no more than 3 years.

Under the *civil* provisions, the statute of limitations runs for 2 years from the discovery of the offense or to 3 years after the act occurred, whichever occurs first.

Case Study: Fraudulent Sale of Securities

Situation: Mr. Thompson, the registered sales agent, *knowingly* omitted the fact that the shares of a company he sold to his client, Mr. Bixby, were downgraded to speculative grade and that their bonds were placed on a credit watch by one of the major credit rating agencies. A month after the sale, the shares became worthless.

Analysis: Mr. Thompson sold these securities to Mr. Bixby in violation of the Uniform Securities Act because he deliberately or knowingly failed to mention material information—information that was important for Mr. Bixby to know in order for him to make an informed investment decision. Mr. Bixby has the right to recover the financial losses that result from the sale.

✓ ***Take Note:*** Under the USA, the actual seller of the securities or the advice is not the only person liable for the violation of the act. Every person who directly or indirectly controls the person who sold the securities or the advice, or is a material aid to the transaction, is also liable to the same extent as the person who conducted the transaction.

Judicial Review of Orders (Appeal)

Any person affected by an order of the **Administrator** may obtain a review of the order in an appropriate court by filing a written petition within 60 days. A copy of the petition must also be served upon the Administrator who then must supply the court with evidence supporting the order. The court may order additional evidence and the Administrator may modify the findings on the basis of this evidence. Filing of an appeal does not automatically act as a stay of the penalty. The order will generally go into effect as issued unless the court rules otherwise. The court has exclusive jurisdiction to affirm, modify, enforce, or set aside the order in whole or in part. The judgment of the court is final.

Quick Quiz 4.5

1. Which of the following statements relating to penalties under the USA is TRUE?

    F   A. Unknowing violation of the USA by an agent is cause for imprisonment under the criminal liability provisions of the act.

        B. A purchaser of a security where a violation of the USA occurred may recover the original purchase price plus legal costs plus interest, less any earnings already received.

    F   C. A seller who notices that a sale was made in violation of the act may offer a right of rescission to the purchaser; this must be accepted within the sooner of two years after notice of the violation or three years after the sale.

    F   D. Any person aggrieved by an order of the Administrator may request an appeal of the order within 15 days which, in effect, functions as a stay of the order during the appeal period.

30 days to offer, appeal 60 days

Answer   1. **B.** *In order to be subject to time in prison, a sales agent must knowingly have violated the USA. A client who purchased a security in violation of the USA may recover the original purchase price plus costs involved in filing a lawsuit. In addition, the purchaser is entitled to interest at a rate stated by the Administrator, less any earnings already received on the investment. The right of rescission must be accepted within 30 days of receipt of the letter of rescission. Although any person aggrieved by an order of the Administrator may request an appeal of the order within 60 days, such appeal does not function as a stay order during the appeal process. The person who is subject of the order must comply with the order during the period unless a stay is granted by the court.*

The Administrative Provisions of the USA HotSheet

USA as Model Legislation:	• USA is not *actual* but *model* legislation for each state's own legislation
NSMIA of 1996:	• Eliminates state and federal registration duplication
Securities Litigation Uniform Standards Act (1998):	• Class actions governed by federal standards
Federal Covered Securities:	• Covered by national, not state, regulation • Includes securities listed on US exchanges, Nasdaq National Market (not SmallCap), issued by investment companies, or sold to qualified purchasers • Includes government and municipal bonds (but not municipal bonds issued within that state)

Administrator:	• State official responsible for the implementation of the USA
Powers of the Administrator:	• Make rules and orders • Conduct investigations and issue subpoenas • Issue cease and desist orders and seek injunctions • Deny, suspend, cancel, or revoke registrations
Fraud:	• Willful misrepresentation for unlawful gain
Civil Liabilities:	• Attorney's costs *plus* losses on investment *plus* interest *minus* any income received
Rescission:	• Right to rescind a transaction in violation of the USA—30 day letter
Criminal Penalties:	• Fines or imprisonment, or both
Statute of Limitations:	• Time limits for bringing suit in a case • **Civil**—3 years from date of sale or of rendering of advice or 2 years after discovering violation, whichever occurs first • **Criminal**—5 years after date of the transaction

Series 63
Unit Test 4

1. If convicted of a willful violation of the Uniform Securities Act, an agent is subject to

    A. imprisonment for 5 years
    B. a fine of $5,000 and/or imprisonment for 3 years
    C. a fine of $10,000
    D. disbarment

2. To protect the public, the Administrator may

    I.   deny a registration if the registrant does not have sufficient experience to function as an agent
    II. limit a registrant's functions to that of a broker/dealer if, in the initial application for registration as an investment adviser, the registrant is not qualified to act as an adviser
    III. take into consideration that the registrant will work under the supervision of a registered investment adviser or broker/dealer in approving a registration
    IV. deny a registration, although denial is not in the public's interest, if it is prudent in view of a change in the state's political composition

    A. I and II only
    B. II and III only
    C. III and IV only
    D. I, II, III and IV

3. Aaron Jones is a client of XYZ Financial Services. Over the past several years, Aaron has been suspicious of possible churning of his account, but has taken no action because account performance has been outstanding. After reviewing his most recent statement, Aaron suspects that excessive transactions have occurred. He consults his attorney who informs him that under the USA, any lawsuit for recovery of damages under the USA must be started within

    A. 1 year of occurrence
    B. 2 years of occurrence
    C. 3 years of occurrence or 2 years of discovery, whichever occurs first
    D. 2 years of occurrence or 3 years of discovery whichever occurs last

4. Which of the following accurately describes a cease and desist order as authorized by the USA?

    A. An order issued by a federal agency to a brokerage firm to stop an advertising campaign
    B. An order by the Administrator to refrain from a practice of business believed by that Administrator to be unfair.
    C. An order issued by a court requiring a business to stop an unfair practice
    D. An order from one brokerage firm to another brokerage firm to refrain from unfair business practices

5. A customer living in one state receives a phone call from an agent in another state. A transaction between the two occurs in yet another state. According to the Uniform Securities Act, under whose jurisdiction does the transaction fall?

    A. Administrator of the state in which the customer lives
    B. Administrator of the state in which the agent is registered
    C. Administrator of the state in which the transaction took place
    D. Administrators of all 3 states involved

6. The Administrator may, by rule,

   A. forbid an adviser from taking custody of client funds
   B. allow an agent to waive provisions of the USA
   C. suspend federal law if the Administrator believes it to be in the public interest
   D. suspend the registration of a federal covered adviser because the contract did not meet the requirements for a state sanctioned investment advisory contract

7. If it is in the public interest, the Uniform Securities Act provides that the state Administrator may deny the registration of a person for all of the following reasons EXCEPT that

   A. the applicant is not qualified owing to lack of experience
   B. a willful violation of the Uniform Securities Act has taken place
   C. the applicant is financially insolvent
   D. the applicant is enjoined temporarily from engaging in the securities business

8. If an agent chooses to appeal an Administrator's order, the agent must file for review of the order with the appropriate court

   A. immediately
   B. within 30 days after the entry of the order
   C. within 60 days after the entry of the order
   D. within 180 days after the entry of the order

9. An Administrator may summarily suspend a registration pending final determination of proceedings under the USA. However, the Administrator may not enter an order without

   I. appropriate prior notice to the applicant as well as the employer or prospective employer of the applicant
   II. opportunity for a hearing
   III. findings of fact and conclusions of law
   IV. prior written acknowledgment of the applicant

   A. I only
   B. I and II only
   C. I, II and III only
   D. I, II, III and IV

10. The Administrator has authority to

   I. issue a cease and desist order without a hearing
   II. issue a cease and desist order only after a hearing
   III. suspend a securities registration upon discovering an officer of the registrant has been convicted of a nonsecurities related crime.
   IV. sentence violators of the USA to 3 years in prison

   A. I only
   B. I and IV only
   C. II and III only
   D. II and IV only

Series 63
Unit Test 4
Answers & Rationale

1.　B.　Under the USA, the maximum penalty is a fine of $5,000 and/or 3 years in jail.

2.　B.　The Administrator can deny, suspend, or revoke a registration for many reasons, but they must be in the interest of the public. The Administrator may not deny the registration simply because it is prudent—it must be in the best interest of the public. The Administrator may determine that an applicant, in his initial application for registration for an investment adviser, is not qualified to act as an adviser and thus limit the registration to that of a broker/dealer and the Administrator can also take into consideration whether the registrant will work under the supervision of a registered investment adviser or broker/dealer when approving an application. Lack of experience is insufficient for denial.

3.　C.　Under the USA, the lawsuit for recovery of damages must commence within 3 years of occurrence of the offense or 2 years of its discovery.

4.　B.　A cease and desist order is a directive from an administrative agency to immediately stop a particular action. The order can come from a federal, state, or judicial body; it is not exclusive to any one. Administrators may issue cease and desist orders with or without a hearing. Brokerage houses cannot issue cease and desist orders to each other.

5.　D.　Under the scope of the Uniform Securities Act, if any part of a transaction occurs in a state, the transaction falls under the jurisdiction of the state Administrator. The transaction is under the control of the Administrator of the state in which the customer lives as the offer was received there, the Administrator of the state in which the agent is calling as the offer was made from that state, and the Administrator of the state in which the transaction took place.

6.　A.　The Administrator has considerable discretion to make rules or issue orders. Specifically, the USA allows the Administrator to prohibit custody by rule. However, the USA does not allow the Administrator to waive provisions of the USA, nor can the Administrator suspend federal law.

7.　A.　If the person qualifies by virtue of training or knowledge, registration cannot be denied for lack of experience only. Registration may be denied if the applicant willfully violates the Uniform Securities Act, is financially insolvent, or has been enjoined from engaging in the securities business.

8.　C.　Under the USA, a registered person has up to 60 days to appeal any disciplinary finding by the state Administrator.

9.　C.　With the exception of those proceedings awaiting final determination, the Administrator must provide an appropriate prior notice to the applicant as well as the employer or prospective employer of the applicant and provide the opportunity for a hearing. In addition, the Administrator may only issue a final stop order after findings of fact and conclusions of law. An applicant is not required to provide written acknowledgement before an order is issued.

10.　A.　The Administrator may issue a cease and desist order without a hearing, but does not have the authority to convict violators of the 1933 Securities Act in criminal prosecutions nor sentence violators of the USA. The Administrator may not suspend a security's registration upon discovering in subsequent years that an officer of the firm has been convicted of a nonsecurities related crime.

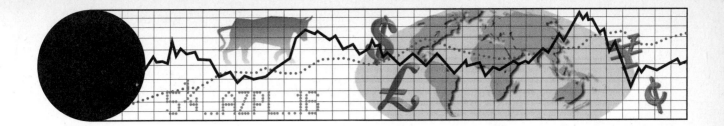

Appendix A

Federal Securities Laws

The following federal laws serve as the regulatory framework for the securities industry.

The Securities Act of 1933

The Securities Act of 1933, also known as the Paper Act, requires companies that intend to sell their securities to the public through interstate commerce or the mail to register the securities with the Securities and Exchange Commission (SEC) by filing a prospectus and a registration statement.

The act requires the full and fair disclosure of relevant information in the prospectus for investors to obtain information necessary to make informed decisions. Its purpose is to prevent fraud in the sale of new issues. The SEC does not review or pass on the investment merit of securities or companies issuing securities.

✓ **Take Note:** Certain issuers of securities are not subject to the registration and filing requirements of the Act of 1933. These **exempt issuers** include the US government, municipalities, nonprofit organizations, and banks.

The Securities Exchange Act of 1934

The 1934 Act created the Securities and Exchange Commission which was given responsibility and authority to regulate the securities markets. The

SEC is made up of five commissioners appointed by the President of the United States and approved by the Senate. The SEC's primary responsibility is to enforce the 1934 act, the major provisions of which address the:

- registration and regulation of the exchanges;
- regulation of credit and margin requirements (currently 50%) set by the Federal Reserve Board (FRB) through Regulation T (Reg T);
- registration of broker/dealers that trade securities on national exchanges or over the counter (OTC);
- registration of persons effecting securities transactions with the public;
- regulation of insider transactions, short sales, and proxies;
- regulation of trading activities;
- regulation of client accounts;
- customer protection rule;
- regulation of the self-regulatory organizations, such as the National Association of Securities Dealers (NASD) and the Municipal Securities Rulemaking Board (MSRB);
- regulation of the OTC market; and
- net capital requirements for broker/dealers.

The SEC has established rules regarding net capital requirements for broker/dealers, hypothecation (pledging) of customers' securities, commingling (mixing) of broker/dealer securities with those of customers, using manipulative and deceptive devices, and broker/dealer recordkeeping.

The SEC enforces the Securities Exchange Act of 1934 and others by providing rules and prescribing penalties for violations. SROs, such as the NASD, are required to assist the SEC in its enforcement practices by establishing rules and trade practices that their member firms must follow. However, the SEC's jurisdiction does not extend to violations of banking rules. The Commission has pre-emptive authority over the rules established by the Uniform Securities Act or state securities Administrators.

In addition to the registration of exchanges, the Act of 1934 requires companies that list securities on those exchanges to register with the SEC. Each listed company must file quarterly statements on Form 10Q and annual statements on Form 10K informing the SEC of its financial status.

✓ **Take Note:** Although some securities are exempt from the registration provisions of the Securities Act of 1933, no securities are exempt from the antifraud provisions of the Act of 1934. Fraudulent practices never can be used in the sale of any security.

Public Utility Holding Company Act of 1935

The Public Utility Holding Company Act requires the registration of all public holding companies engaged in the electric utility business or in the retail distribution of gas unless exempted by rule or order.

Maloney Act of 1938

The Maloney Act, an amendment to the Securities Exchange Act of 1934, authorized the establishment and registration of national self-regulatory organizations such as the NASD. Broker/dealers must be members of such organizations to transact securities business.

Trust Indenture Act of 1939

The Trust Indenture Act of 1939 requires that each public issue of debt securities exceeding $5 million in a 12-month period be issued under a trust indenture. A trustee must ensure that the indenture includes specific provisions for the protection of the bondholders.

Investment Advisers Act of 1940

The Investment Advisers Act of 1940 provides for the registration and regulation of investment advisers. It prohibits deceptive practices between advisers and their clients and requires that advisers make certain disclosures to prospective clients, including their fees, backgrounds, and methods of transacting business.

Investment Company Act of 1940

The Investment Company Act of 1940 provides for SEC registration and regulation of investment companies, including open-end investment companies (mutual funds), closed-end investment companies, unit investment trusts (UITs), and insurance company separate accounts.

Securities Investor Protection Act of 1970

The Securities Investor Protection Corporation (SIPC) was established in 1970 with the passage of the Securities Investor Protection Act. The purpose of the act is to protect customers of securities firms that go bankrupt.

SIPC oversees the liquidation of bankrupt firms and provides coverage of up to $500,000 in cash and securities to each customer of the firms.

Insider Trading and Securities Fraud Enforcement Act of 1988

The Insider Trading and Securities Fraud Enforcement Act of 1988 expanded the definition of, and the liabilities and penalties for, the unlawful use of non-public information prohibited by the Securities Exchange Act of 1934. An insider is any person who has access to nonpublic information about a corporation. Insiders may not use inside information as a basis for personal trading or benefit until that information has been made public.

Written Supervisory Procedures

All broker/dealers must establish, maintain, and enforce written supervisory procedures specifically prohibiting the use of material nonpublic information by all persons interested in, affiliated with, or in any way engaged in the broker/dealers' securities-related activities.

Criminal Penalties

The criminal penalties for violations of securities laws were increased through the 1988 Insider Trading and Securities Fraud Enforcement Act. Persons convicted of violating the act can be fined the greater of $1 million or 300% of profits received or losses avoided, sentenced to prison for up to 10 years, or both.

Telephone Consumer Protection Act of 1991

The Telephone Consumer Protection Act of 1991 (TCPA), administered by the Federal Communications Commission (FCC), was enacted to protect consumers from unwanted telephone solicitations, including recorded auto-dialer solicitations and facsimile machine and modem (email) solicitations.

The act requires any organization that performs telemarketing (in particular, cold calling) to:

- maintain a *Do-Not-Call* list of customers who do not want to be called and keep a prospective customer's name on the list for 10 years from the time the request is made;
- institute a written policy, available on demand, regarding maintenance procedures for the *Do-Not-Call* list;
- train reps to use the list;
- ensure that reps acknowledge and immediately record the names and telephone numbers of customers who ask not to be called again; and
- call the homes of prospective customers only between the hours of 8:00 am and 9:00 pm in the prospective customers' time zones.

✓ **Take Note:** This act also applies to broker/dealers.

National Securities Markets Improvement Act of 1996

The National Securities Markets Improvement Act of 1996 (NSMIA) expanded the SEC's role to include improvement and oversight of:

- market efficiency;
- competition in the securities industry;
- capital formation;
- elimination of regulations that no longer serve the public interest; and
- elimination of the dual state and federal regulation.

Under NSMIA, the SEC eliminated the dual regulation of securities by defining those securities covered by federal law as "federal covered securities" which no longer can be subject to state registration.

Because of its role in coordinating the activities of the various securities regulators, this act sometimes is referred to as the Coordination Act.

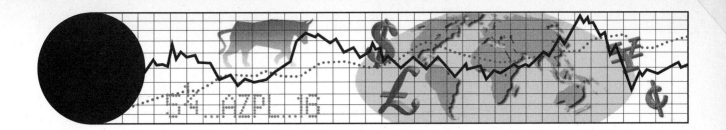

Appendix B

NASAA's Statement of Policy

Dishonest or Unethical Business Practices by Broker/Dealers and Agents in Connection with Investment Company Shares

**NASAA Broker/
Dealer Sales Practice
Committee
Adopted 4/27/97**

Any broker/dealer or agent who engages in one or more of the following practices shall be deemed to have engaged in "dishonest or unethical practices in the securities business" as used in Section 204 of the Uniform Securities Act and such conduct may constitute grounds for denial, suspension, or revocation of registration or such other action authorized by statute.

A. Sales Load Communications:

1. In connection with the solicitation of investment company shares, failing to adequately disclose to a customer all sales charges, including asset based and contingent deferred sales charges, which may be imposed with respect to the purchase, retention or redemption of such shares.

2. In connection with the solicitation of investment company shares, stating or implying to a customer that the shares are sold without a commission, are "no load," or have "no sales charge" if there is associated with the purchase of the shares: (i) a front-end load; (ii) a contingent deferred sales load; (iii) a SEC Rule 12b-1 fee or a service fee if such fees in total exceed .25% of average net fund assets per year; or (iv) in the case of closed-end investment company shares, underwriting fees, commissions, or other offering expenses.

3. In connection with the solicitation of investment company shares, failing to disclose to any customer any relevant: (i) sales charge discount on the purchase of shares in dollar amounts at or above a breakpoint; or (ii) letter of intent feature, if available, which will reduce the sales charges.

4. In connection with the solicitation of investment company shares, recommending to a customer the purchase of a specific class of investment company shares in connection with a multi-class sales charge or fee arrangement without reasonable grounds to believe that the sales charge or fee arrangement associated with such class of shares is suitable and appropriate based on the customer's investment objectives, financial situation, other securities holdings, and the associated transaction or other fees.

B. Recommendations:

1. In connection with the solicitation of investment company shares, recommending to a customer the purchase of investment company shares which results in the customer simultaneously holding shares in different investment company portfolios having similar investment objectives and policies without reasonable grounds to believe that such recommendation is suitable and appropriate based on the customer's investment objectives, financial situation and other securities holdings and any associated transaction charges or other fees.

2. In connection with the solicitation of investment company shares, recommending to a customer the liquidation or redemption of investment company shares for the purpose of purchasing shares in a different investment company portfolio having similar investment objectives and policies without reasonable grounds to believe that such recommendation is suitable and appropriate based on the customer's investment objectives, financial situation and other securities holdings and any associated transaction charges or other fees.

C. Disclosure:

1. In connection with the solicitation of investment company shares, stating or implying to a customer the fund's current yield or income without disclosing the fund's most recent average annual return, calculated in a manner prescribed in SEC Form N-1A, for one, five and ten year periods and fully explaining the difference between current yield and total return; provided, however, that the fund's registration statement under the Securities Act of 1933 has been in effect for less than one, five, or ten years, the time during which the registration statement was in effect shall be substituted for the periods otherwise prescribed.

2. In connection with the solicitation of investment company shares, stating or implying to a customer that the investment performance of an investment company portfolio is comparable to that of a savings account, certificate of deposit or other bank deposit account without disclosing to the

customer that the shares are not insured or otherwise guaranteed by the FDIC or any other government agency and the relevant differences regarding risk, guarantees, fluctuation of principal and/or return, and any other factors which are necessary to ensure that such comparisons are fair, complete and not misleading.

3. In connection with the solicitation of investment company shares, stating or implying to a customer the existence of insurance, credit quality, guarantees or similar features regarding securities held, or proposed to be held, in the investment company's portfolio without disclosing to the customer other kinds of relevant investment risks, including but not limited to, interest rate, market, political, liquidity, or currency exchange risks, which may adversely affect investment performance and result in loss and/or fluctuation of principal notwithstanding the creditworthiness of such portfolio securities.

4. In connection with the solicitation of investment company shares, stating or implying to a customer: (i) that the purchase of such shares shortly before an ex-dividend date is advantageous to such customer unless there are specific, clearly described tax or other advantages to the customer; or (ii) that a distribution of long-term capital gains by an investment company is part of the income yield from an investment in such shares.

5. In connection with the solicitation of investment company shares, making: (i) projections of future performance; (ii) statements not warranted under existing circumstances; or (iii) statements based upon non-public information.

D. Prospectus:

In connection with the solicitation of investment company shares, the delivery of a prospectus, in and of itself, shall not be dispositive that the broker/dealer or agent provided the customer full and fair disclosure.

E. Definitions:

For the purpose of this rule, the following terms shall mean:

1. "Recommend": any affirmative act or statement that endorses, solicits, requests, or commends a securities transaction to a customer or any affirmative act or statement that solicits, requests, commands, importunes or intentionally aids such person to engage in such conduct.

2. "Solicitation": any oral, written or other communication used to offer or sell investment company shares excluding any proxy statement, report to shareholders, or other disclosure document relating to a security covered under Section 18(b)(2) of the Securities Act of 1933 that is required to be

and is filed with the Commission or any national securities organization registered under Section 15A of the Securities Exchange Act of 1934.

(Note: This Statement of Policy is intended to supplement, not supplant, the NASAA Statement of Policy Regarding the Dishonest or Unethical Business Practices.)

Unethical Business Practices of Investment Advisers

Amended 4/27/1997, Adopted in 1985

A person who is an investment adviser or a federal covered adviser is a fiduciary and has a duty to act primarily for the benefit of its clients. The provisions of this subsection apply to federal covered advisers to the extent that the conduct alleged is fraudulent, deceptive, or as otherwise permitted by the National Securities Markets Improvement Act of 1996 (Pub. L. No. 104-290). While the extent and nature of this duty varies according to the nature of the relationship between an investment adviser and its clients and the circumstances of each case, an investment adviser or a federal covered adviser shall not engage in unethical business practices, including the following:

1. Recommending to a client to whom supervisory, management or consulting services are provided the purchase, sale or exchange of any security without reasonable grounds to believe that the recommendation is suitable for the client on the basis of information furnished by the client after reasonable inquiry concerning the client's investment objectives, financial situation and needs, and any other information known by the investment adviser.

2. Exercising any discretionary power in placing an order for the purchase or sale of securities for a client without obtaining written discretionary authority from the client within ten (10) business days after the date of the first transaction placed pursuant to oral discretionary authority, unless the discretionary power relates solely to the price at which, or the time when, an order involving a definite amount of a specified security shall be executed, or both.

3. Inducing trading in a client's account that is excessive in size or frequency in view of the financial resources, investment objectives and character of the account in light of the fact that an adviser in such situations can directly benefit from the number of securities transactions effected in a client's account. The rule appropriately forbids an excessive number of transaction orders to be induced by an adviser for a "customer's account."

4. Placing an order to purchase or sell a security for the account of a client without authority to do so.

5. Placing an order to purchase or sell a security for the account of a client upon instruction of a third party without first having obtained a written third-party trading authorization from the client.

6. Borrowing money or securities from a client unless the client is a broker/dealer, an affiliate of the investment adviser, or a financial institution engaged in the business of loaning funds.

7. Loaning money to a client unless the investment adviser is a financial institution engaged in the business of loaning funds or the client is an affiliate of the investment adviser.

8. To misrepresent to any advisory client, or prospective advisory client, the qualifications of the investment adviser or any employee of the investment adviser, or to misrepresent the nature of the advisory services being offered or fees to be charged for such service, or to omit to state a material fact necessary to make the statements made regarding qualifications, services or fees, in light of the circumstances under which they are made, not misleading.

9. Providing a report or recommendation to any advisory client prepared by someone other than the adviser without disclosing that fact. (This prohibition does not apply to a situation where the adviser uses published research reports or statistical analyses to render advice or where an adviser orders such a report in the normal course of providing service.)

10. Charging a client an unreasonable advisory fee.

11. Failing to disclose to clients in writing before any advice is rendered any material conflict of interest relating to the adviser or any of its employees which could reasonably be expected to impair the rendering of unbiased and objective advice including:

    (a) Compensation arrangements connected with advisory services to clients which are in addition to compensation from such clients for such services; and

    (b) Charging a client an advisory fee for rendering advice when a commission for executing securities transactions pursuant to such advice will be received by the adviser or its employees.

12. Guaranteeing a client that a specific result will be achieved (gain or no loss) with advice which will be rendered.

13. Publishing, circulating or distributing any advertisement which does not comply with Rule 206 (4)-1 under the Investment Advisers Act of 1940.

14. Disclose the identity, affairs, or investments of any client unless required by law to do so, or unless consented to by the client.

15. Taking any action, directly or indirectly, with respect to those securities or funds in which any client has any beneficial interest, where the investment adviser has custody or possession of such securities or funds when

the advisor's action is subject to and does not comply with the requirements of Reg. 2O6 (4)-2 under the Investment Advisers Act of 1940.

16. Entering into, extending or renewing any investment advisory contract unless such contract is in writing and discloses, in substance, the services to be provided, the term of the contract, the advisory fee, the formula for computing the fee, the amount of prepaid fee to be returned in the event of contract termination or nonperformance, whether the contract grants discretionary power to the adviser and that no assignment of such contract shall be made by the investment adviser without the consent of the other party to the contract.

17. Failing to establish, maintain, and enforce written policies and procedures reasonably designed to prevent the misuse of material nonpublic information contrary to the provisions of Section 204A of the Investment Advisers Act of 1940.

18. Entering into, extending, or renewing any advisory contract contrary to the provisions of Section 205 of the Investment Advisers Act of 1940. This provision shall apply to all advisers registered or required to be registered under this act, notwithstanding whether such adviser would be exempt from federal registration pursuant to Section 203 (b) of the Investment Advisers Act of 1940.

19. To indicate, in an advisory contract, any condition, stipulation, or provisions binding any person to waive compliance with any provision of this act or of the Investment Advisers Act of 1940, or any other practice contrary to the provisions of Section 215 of the Investment Advisers Act of 1940.

20. Engaging in any act, practice, or course of business which is fraudulent, deceptive, or manipulative in contrary to the provisions of Section 206 (4) of the Investment Advisers Act of 1940, notwithstanding the fact that such investment adviser is not registered or required to be registered under Section 203 of the Investment Advisers Act of 1940.

21. Engaging in conduct or any act, indirectly or through or by any other person, which would be unlawful for such person to do directly under the provisions of this act or any rule or regulation thereunder. The conduct set forth above is not inclusive. Engaging in other conduct such as nondisclosure, incomplete disclosure, or deceptive practices shall be deemed an unethical business practice.

The federal statutory and regulatory provisions referenced herein shall apply to investment advisers and federal covered advisers, to the extent permitted by the National Securities Markets Improvement Act of 1996 (Pub. L. No. 104-290).

Dishonest or Unethical Business Practices of Broker/Dealers and Agents

Adopted May 23, 1983

HIGH STANDARDS AND JUST PRINCIPLES. Each broker/dealer and agent shall observe high standards of commercial honor and just and equitable principles of trade in the conduct of their business. Acts and practices, including but not limited to the following, are considered contrary to such standards and may constitute grounds for denial, suspension or revocation of registration or such other action authorized by statute.

1. Broker/Dealers

a. Engaging in a pattern of unreasonable and unjustifiable delays in the delivery of securities purchased by any of its customers and/or in the payment upon request of free credit balances reflecting completed transactions of any of its customers.

b. Inducing trading in a customer's account which is excessive in size or frequency in view of the financial resources and character of the account.

c. Recommending to a customer the purchase, sale or exchange of any security without reasonable grounds to believe that such transaction or recommendation is suitable for the customer based upon reasonable inquiry concerning the customer's investment objectives, financial situation and needs, and any other relevant information known by the broker/dealer.

d. Executing a transaction on behalf of a customer without authorization to do so.

e. Exercising any discretionary power in effecting a transaction for a customer's account without first obtaining written discretionary authority from the customer, unless the discretionary power relates solely to the time and/or price for the executing of orders.

f. Executing any transaction in a margin account without securing from the customer a properly executed written margin agreement promptly after the initial transaction in the account.

g. Failing to segregate customers' free securities or securities held in safekeeping.

h. Hypothecating a customer's securities without having a lien thereon unless the broker/dealer secures from the customer a properly executed written consent promptly after the initial transaction, except as permitted by Rules of the Securities and Exchange Commission.

i. Entering into a transaction with or for a customer at a price not reasonably related to the current market price of the security or receiving an unreasonable commission or profit.

j. Failing to furnish to a customer purchasing securities in an offering, no later than the due date of confirmation of the transaction, either a final prospectus or a preliminary prospectus and an additional document, which together include all information set forth in the final prospectus.

k. Charging unreasonable and inequitable fees for services performed, including miscellaneous services such as collection of monies due for principal, dividends or interest, exchange or transfer of securities, appraisals, safekeeping, or custody of securities and other services related to its securities business.

l. Offering to buy from or sell to any person any security at a stated price unless such broker/dealer is prepared to purchase or sell, as the case may be, at such price and under such conditions as are stated at the time of such offer to buy or sell.

m. Representing that a security is being offered to a customer "at the market" or a price relevant to the market price unless such broker/dealer knows or has reasonable grounds to believe that a market for such security exists other than that made, created or controlled by such broker/dealer, or by any such person for whom he is acting or with whom he is associated in such distribution, or any person controlled by, controlling or under common control with such broker/dealer.

n. Effecting any transaction in, or inducing the purchase or sale of, any security by means of any manipulative, deceptive or fraudulent device, practice, plan, program, design or contrivance, which may include but not be limited to:

(1) Effecting any transaction in a security which involves no change in the beneficial ownership thereof;

(2) Entering an order or orders for the purchase or sale of any security with the knowledge that an order or orders of substantially the same size, at substantially the same time and substantially the same price, for the sale of any such security, has been or will be entered by or for the same or different parties for the purpose of creating a false or misleading appearance of active trading in the security or a false or misleading appearance with respect to the market for the security; provided, however, nothing in this subsection shall prohibit a broker/dealer from entering bona fide agency cross transactions for its customers; or

(3) Effecting, alone or with one or more other persons, a series of transactions in any security creating actual or apparent active trading in such security or raising or depressing the price of such security, for the purpose of inducing the purchase or sale of such security by others.

o. Guaranteeing a customer against loss in any securities account of such customer carried by the broker/dealer or in any securities transaction effected by the broker/dealer or in any securities transaction effected by the broker/dealer with or for such customer.

p. Publishing or circulating, or causing to be published or circulated, any notice, circular, advertisement, newspaper article, investment service, or communication of any kind which purports to report any transaction as a purchase or sale of any security unless such broker/dealer believes that such transaction was a bona fide purchase or sale or such security; or which purports to quote the bid price or asked price for any security, unless such broker/dealer believes that such quotation represents a bona fide bid for, or offer of, such security.

q. Using any advertising or sales presentation in such a fashion as to be deceptive or misleading. An example of such practice would be a distribution of any nonfactual data, material or presentation based on conjecture, unfounded or unrealistic claims or assertions in any brochure, flyer, or display by words, pictures, graphs or otherwise designed to supplement, detract from, supersede or defeat the purpose or effect of any prospectus or disclosure.

r. Failing to disclose that the broker/dealer is controlled by, controlling, affiliated with or under common control with the issuer of any security before entering into any contract with or for a customer for the purchase or sale of such security, the existence of such control to such customer, and if such disclosure is not made in writing, it shall be supplemented by the giving or sending of written disclosure at or before the completion of the transaction.

s. Failing to make a bona fide public offering of all of the securities allotted to a broker/dealer for distribution, whether acquired as an underwriter, a selling group member, or from a member participating in the distribution as an underwriter or selling group member.

t. Failure or refusal to furnish a customer, upon reasonable request, information to which he is entitled, or to respond to a formal written request or complaint.

2. Agents

a. Engaging in the practice of lending or borrowing money or securities from a customer, or acting as a custodian for money, securities or an executed stock power of a customer.

b. Effecting securities transactions not recorded on the regular books or records of the broker/dealer which the agent represents, unless the transactions are authorized in writing by the broker/dealer prior to execution of the transaction.

c. Establishing or maintaining an account containing fictitious information in order to execute transactions which would otherwise be prohibited.

d. Sharing directly or indirectly in profits or losses in the account of any customer without the written authorization of the customer and the broker/dealer which the agent represents.

e. Dividing or otherwise splitting the agent's commissions, profits or other compensation from the purchase or sale of securities with any person not also registered as an agent for the same broker/dealer, or for a broker/dealer under direct or indirect common control.

f. Engaging in conduct specified in Subsection 1.b, c, d, e, f, i, j, n, o, p, or q.

CONDUCT NOT INCLUSIVE. The conduct set forth above is not inclusive. Engaging in other conduct such as forgery, embezzlement, nondisclosure, incomplete disclosure or misstatement of material facts, or manipulative or deceptive practices shall also be grounds for denial, suspension or revocation of registration.

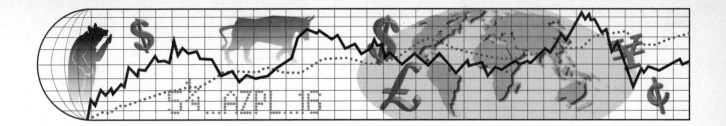

Glossary

A

accredited investor Any institution or individual meeting minimum net worth requirements for the purchase of securities qualifying under the Regulation D registration exemption, as defined in Rule 502 of Regulation D.

An accredited investor generally is accepted to be one who:

- has a net worth of $1 million or more; or
- has had an annual income of $200,000 or more in each of the two most recent years (or $300,000 jointly with a spouse) and who has a reasonable expectation of reaching the same income level in the current year.

administrator (1) The official or agency administering the securities laws of a state. (2) A person authorized by a court of law to liquidate the estate of an intestate decedent.

advertisement Any material designed for use by newspapers, magazines, radio, television, telephone recording, or any other public medium to solicit business. The firm using advertising has little control over the type of individuals being exposed to the advertising. *See also* sales literature.

advertising prospectus An investment company prospectus that includes the fund's performance data, as well as standardized information contained in the summary prospectus.

affiliate Any person directly or indirectly owning, controlling, or holding (with power to vote) 10% or more of the outstanding voting securities of another person. Also, any officer, director, or partner of another entity for which such person acts in such capacity.

When used with respect to a member or sponsor, *affiliate* means any person who controls, is controlled by, or is under control with such member or sponsor and includes:

- any partner, officer, or director (or any person performing similar functions) of such member or sponsor or a person who beneficially owns 50% or more of the equity interest in, or who has the power to vote 50% or more of the voting interest in, such member or sponsor; or
- any person who beneficially owns or has the right to acquire 10% or more of the equity interest in or who has the power to vote 10% or more of the voting interest in, such member or sponsor, or a person who beneficially owns 50% or more of the voting interest in, or who has the power to vote 50% or more of the voting interest in, such member or sponsor.

agent (1) An individual acting for the accounts of others; also, any person licensed by a state as a life insurance agent. *Syn.* broker. (2) A securities salesperson who represents a broker/dealer or an issuer when selling or trying to sell securities to the investing public. This individual is considered an agent whether he actually receives or simply solicits orders. An agent is anyone who receives an order while representing a broker/dealer.

assignment (1) A document accompanying or part of a stock certificate that is signed by the person named on the certificate for the purpose of transferring the certificate's title to another person's name. (2) The act of identifying and notifying an account holder that an option held short in that account has been exercised by the option owner.

associated person of a member (AP) Any employee, manager, director, officer, or partner of a member broker/dealer or another entity (issuer, bank, etc.) or any person controlling, controlled by, or in common control with that member is considered an associated person of that member.

B

blue-sky To qualify a securities offering in a particular state.

blue-sky laws The commonly-used for state regulations governing the securities industry.

broker (1) An individual or a firm that charges a fee or commission for executing buy and sell orders submitted by another individual or firm. (2) The role of a broker firm when it acts as an agent for a customer and charges the customer a commission for its services. *See also* agent.

broker/dealer (1) An individual or a firm that charges a fee or commission for executing buy and sell orders submitted by another individual or firm. (2) The role of a broker firm when it acts as an agent for a customer and charges the customer a commission for its services.

The term "broker/dealer" is defined in the Uniform Securities Act so that it can be determined who must register in the state as a broker/dealer. If the person does not fall under the definition of broker/dealer as defined by the law, the registration process is not necessary. The following persons are not classified as broker/dealers.
- Agents (registered representatives)
- Issuers
- Banks, savings institutions or trust companies
- Persons who have no place of business in the state and who: (a) effect securities transactions in the state exclusively through the issuers of the securities, other broker/dealers, or financial institutions (banks, savings institutions, trust companies, insurance companies, and investment companies) or (b) directs an offer in this state to an existing customer who has less than 30 days' temporary residency in the state where the offer is received.

C

churning A prohibited practice in which a salesperson effects transactions in a customer's account which are excessive in size and/or frequency in relation to the size and character of the account.

commission A broker's fee for handling transactions for a client in an agency capacity.

consent to service of process A legal agreement entered into by all registrants, whereby the administrator is given the power to accept legal papers on behalf of the registrant.

custodian A commercial bank or trust company that holds monies and securities owned by an investment company in safekeeping.

custody Maintaining possession of a customer's money and/or securities. Many states prohibit investment advisors from keeping custody. The others require the adviser to notify the Administrator if it intends to do so.

D

dealer The role of a brokerage firm when it acts as a principal in a particular trade. A firm is acting as a dealer when it buys or sells a security for its own account and at its own risk and then charges the customer a markup or markdown. Any person who is engaged in the business of buying and selling securities for her own account either directly or through a broker, and who is not a bank, is considered a dealer. *Syn.* principal.

debenture An unsecured long-term debt offering by a corporation, promising only the general assets as protection for these creditors.

discretion The authority for someone other than the beneficial owner of an account to make investment decisions for that account regarding the security, the number of shares or units, and whether to buy or sell. Decisions concerning only timing and price do not constitute discretion.

discretionary account An account in which the customer authorizes in writing a broker/dealer or investment adviser to use his judgement in buying and selling securities, including selection, timing, amount, and price. Judgement as to time and/or price only is not considered discretion.

E

effective date The date on which a security can be offered publicly if no stop order is submitted to the issuer by the Administrator.

exempt security A security exempt from the registration requirements (although not from the antifraud requirements) of the Securities Act of 1933 (e.g., U.S. government and municipal securities).

exempt transaction A transaction exempt from registration, sales literature, and advertising requirements under the Uniform Securities Act. Examples of exempt transactions include:
- isolated nonissuer transactions;
- nonissuer transactions in outstanding securities (normal market trading);
- transactions with financial institutions (banks, savings institutions, trust companies, insurance companies, pension or profit-sharing plans, broker/dealers, etc.);
- unsolicited transactions;
- fiduciary transactions;
- private placement transactions;
- transactions between an issuer and its underwriters; and
- transactions with an issuer's employees, partners or directors if no commission is paid directly or indirectly for the soliciting.

Exemption from the act's registration and advertising requirements does not mean that a transaction is exempt from the act's antifraud provisions.

F

federal covered adviser An adviser regulated under the Investment Adviser's Act of 1940 or other federal legislation.

fidelity bond *See* surety bond.

fiduciary A person legally appointed and authorized to represent another person and act on their behalf.

fraud The deliberate concealment, misrepresentation, or omission of material information or the truth to deceive or manipulate another party for unlawful or unfair gain.

G

government security An obligation of the US government, backed by the full faith and credit of the government, and regarded as the highest grade or safest issue (i.e., default risk-free). The US government issues short-term Treasury bills, medium-term Treasury notes and long-term Treasury bonds.

guaranteed Securities that have a guarantee, usually from a source other than the issuer, as to the payment of principal, interest or dividends.

I

inside information Material and nonpublic information obtained or used by a person for the purpose of trading in securities. *See also* material fact.

insider Any person who has nonpublic knowledge (material information) about a corporation. Insiders include directors, officers, and stockholders who own more than 10% of any class of equity security of a corporation.

institutional account An account held for the benefit of others. Examples include banks, trusts, pension and profit-sharing plans, mutual funds, and insurance companies.

institutional investor A person or an organization that trades securities in large enough share quantities or dollar amounts that it qualifies for preferential treatment and lower trade costs (commissions). Institutional investors are covered by fewer protective regulations because it is assumed that they are more knowledgeable and better able to protect themselves.

investment adviser Any person who, for compensation (a flat fee or a percentage of assets managed), offers investment advice. For investment companies, the adviser has the day-to-day responsibility of investing the cash and securities held in a mutual fund's portfolio. The adviser must adhere to the objectives as stated in the fund's prospectus. This definition includes persons who issue written reports or analyses for compensation. The term *investment adviser* does not include:
- institutions such as banks, savings institutions, or trust companies;
- professionals such as lawyers, accountants or teachers whose performance of these services is solely incidental to the practice of their profession;

- broker/dealers that offer investment portfolio advice as part of their business of being broker/dealers and that receive no special compensation for that service;
- publishers of any financial publication of general, regular, and paid circulation; however, a person who sells subscriptions to investment advisory publications (market letters) is considered an investment adviser under the USA;
- persons whose investment advice relates only to U.S. government securities and certain municipal securities; and
- persons having no place of business within the state and whose activities are limited to (a) professional clients (institutions) or (b) a very few solicitations or sales to clients other than those mentioned above. (e.g., less than six clients in any 12 consecutive months).

The term *investment adviser* can exclude any person that the state Administrator of the USA decides not to include.

investment adviser representative   Any partner, officer, director or other individual employed by or associated with an investment adviser who (1) gives investment advice or makes recommendations, (2) manages client accounts or portfolios, (3) determines which investment recommendations or advice should be given, (4) offers or sells investment advisory services, or (5) supervises employees involved in any of these activities.

Investment Advisers Act of 1940   Legislation passed by Congress that requires certain investment advisers to register as such with the SEC and to abide by the Investment Advisers Act of 1940 and all other applicable federal acts.

investment company   A company engaged primarily in the business of investing and trading in securities, including face-amount certificate companies, unit investment trusts, and management companies.

Investment Company Act of 1940   Congressional legislation enacted to regulate investment companies that requires any investment company in interstate commerce to register with the SEC.

issuer   (1) The corporation, government or other entitiy that offers its securities for sale. (2) According to the USA, any person who issues or proposes to issue any security.

When a corporation or municipality raises additional capital through an offering of securities, that corporation or municipality is the issuer of those securities. An issuer transaction is also called a **primary transaction**.

M

market maker (principal)   A dealer willing to accept the risk of holding securities to facilitate trading in a particular security(ies).

material fact   Information required to be included in a registration statement that a knowledgeable investor would deem significant in making an investment determination. *See also* inside information.

municipal security   A debt security issued by a state, a municipality, or another subdivision (such as a school, a park, or a sanitary or some other local taxing district) to raise money to finance its capital expenditures. Such expenditures might include the construction of highways, public works, or school buildings.

N

net capital   Liquid capital (cash and assets readily convertible into cash) maintained by a broker/dealer.

nonissuer   A person other than the issuer of a security. In a nonissuer securities transaction, for example, the issuer is not one of the parties in the transaction, and the transaction therefore is not, according to the law, directly or indirectly for the benefit of the issuer. When the USA refers to a nonissuer transaction, it is referring to a transaction in which the proceeds of the sale go to the selling stockholder. Most nonissuer transactions also are called **secondary transactions**.

notice filing   Procedure under the Uniform Securities Act whereby an issuer notifies state securities administrators of federal registration.

O

offer   (1) An indication by an investor, a trader or a dealer of a willingness to sell a security or commodity. (2) Under the USA, every attempt to solicit a purchase or sale in a security for value.

P

person   An individual, a corporation, a partnership, an association, a fund, a joint stock company, an unincorporated organization, a trust in which the interests of the beneficiaries are evidenced by a security, a government, or a political subdivision of a government.

private investment company An unregistered investment company whose investment objective is to raise capital for business ventures. Qualified purchasers are eligible to invest in private investment companies.

private placement The USA's private placement provision allows an exemption from full state registration for a security that is sold in that state to no more than 10 noninstitutional investors.

prospectus The legal document that must be given to every investor who purchases registered securities in an offering. It describes the details of the company and the particular offering. *Syn.* final prospectus.

R

registered investment company An investment company, such as an open-end management company (mutual fund) or closed-end management company, that is registered with the SEC and exempt from state registration and regulation.

registered representative All associated persons engaged in the investment banking and securities business for NASD registration and exam and licensing purposes. This includes:
- assistant officers (who are not principals);
- individuals who supervise, solicit, or conduct business in securities; and
- individuals who train people to supervise, solicit, or conduct business in securities.

Anyone who is not a principal and not engaged in clerical or brokerage administration is subject to registration and exam licensing as a registered representative—except for foreign associates.

registration by coordination A security is eligible for blue-sky registration by coordination in a state if the issuer files for registration of that security under the Securities Act of 1933 and files duplicates of the registration documents with the state Administrator. The state registration becomes effective at the same time the federal registration statement becomes effective.

registration by filing A security is eligible for blue-sky registration by filing in a state if the issuer files for registration of that security under the Securities Act of 1933, meets minimum net worth and other requirements, and notifies the state of this eligibility by filing certain documents with the state Administrator. The state registration becomes effective at the same time the federal registration statement becomes effective.

registration by qualification A security is eligible for blue-sky registration by qualification in a state if the issuer files registration documents for that security with the state Administrator; meets minimum net worth, disclosure, and other requirements; and files appropriate registration fees. The state registration becomes effective when the Administrator so orders.

registration statement Before nonexempt securities can be offered to the public, they require registration under the Securities Act of 1933. The registration statement must disclose all pertinent information concerning the issuer and the offering. This statement is submitted to the SEC in accordance with the requirements of the 1933 Act.

S

sales literature Any written material used to help sell a product and distributed by the firm in a controlled manner. *See also* advertisement

Securities Act of 1933 The federal legislation requiring the full and fair disclosure of all material information about the issuance of new securities.

Securities and Exchange Commission (SEC) The commission, created by Congress to protect investors, that enforces the Securities Act of 1933, the Securities Exchange Act of 1934, the Trust Indenture Act of 1939, the Investment Company Act of 1940, the Investment Advisers Act of 1940, and other securities laws.

Securities Exchange Act of 1934 The federal legislation establishing the Securities and Exchange Commission that regulates securities exchanges and over-the-counter markets and that protects investors from unfair and inequitable practices.

security Under the Act of 1934, any note, stock, bond, investment contract, debenture, certificate of interest in profit-sharing or partnership agreement, certificate of deposit, collateral trust certificate, preorganization certificate, option on a security, or other instrument of investment commonly known as a **security**.

Also categorized as securities are interests in oil and gas drilling programs, real estate condominiums and cooperatives, farmland or animals, commodity option contracts, whiskey warehouse receipts, multilevel distributorship arrangements, and merchandising marketing programs.

In general, a security can be defined as any piece of securitized paper that can be traded for value, except an insurance policy or a fixed annuity. As established by the federal courts, the basic test for determining whether a specific investment falls within the definition of security is whether the investor invests his money in a common enterprise and is led to expect profits from the managerial efforts of the promoter or a third party.

self-regulatory organization (SRO) An entity that is accountable to the SEC for the enforcement of federal securities laws, as well as for the supervision of securities practices, within an assigned field of jurisdiction.

sell The act of conveying ownership of a security or other property for money or other value; every contract to sell a security or an interest in a security. Sales include the following.

- Any security given or delivered with, or as a bonus for, any purchase of securities is considered to have been offered and sold for value.
- A gift of assessable stock is considered to involve an offer and sale.
- Every sale or offer of a warrant or right to purchase or subscribe to another security is considered to include an offer of the other security.

Sales do not include bona fide pledges or loans or stock dividends if nothing of value is given by the stockholders for the dividend.

surety bond (1) A bond required for all employees, officers and partners of member firms to protect clients against acts of misplacement, fraudulent trading and check forgery. (2) The blanket surety bond that indemnifies against losses due to check forgery, lost securities, or fraudulent trading that every member firm required to join the Securities Investor Protection Corporation (that is, any firm doing business with the public) must purchase and maintain. *Syn.* fidelity bond.

T

transfer agent A person or an organization responsible for recording the names of registered stockholders and the number of shares owned, seeing that the certificates are signed by the appropriate corporate officers, affixing the corporate seal, and delivering the securities to the transferee.

U

underwriter The entity responsible for marketing stocks, bonds, mutual fund shares, etc.

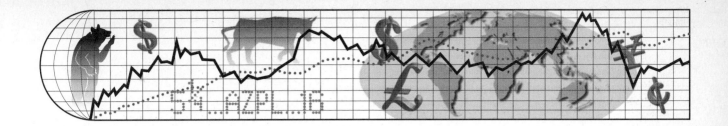

Index

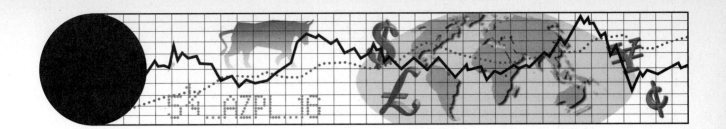

HotSheets

Registration of Persons HotSheet

Person:
- Individual, company, association, or government

Broker/Dealer Registration:
- Must register in state where business is done unless exempt
- Effective after Administrator notification; expires December 31

Exempt from State Registration as a Broker/Dealer:
- Banks, savings institutions, other financial institutions, agents, issuers
- Broker/dealers with no office in state only doing business with institutions
- Broker/dealers registered in another state transacting business with a current client passing through a different state

Exemptions from Agent Registration:
- Represents issuer in exempt transaction
- Represents issuer in exempt securities
- Represents issuer in sale of employee benefits plans
- Must not receive compensation that is sale related

Agent Registration:
- Agents must be registered in state of residence of the client where securities are offered, and where securities are sold
- Agents who represent broker/dealers must be registered if they sell exempt or nonexempt securities
- Broker/dealers can only employ registered agents
- Agents who represent issuers generally must be registered if they sell nonexempt securities
- Effective after Administrator notification, no later than noon of the 30th day; expires December 31
- Notification by agent & old & new broker/dealer for employment change
- Notification by state registered investment adviser or investment adviser representative of federal covered adviser for employment change
- Automatic registration of partners, officers, and directors when new broker/dealers and investment advisers register

Investment Adviser Registration:
- Federally registered if adviser manages more than $30 million
- State registered if adviser manages less than $25 million
- Choice between federal and state if adviser manages between $25 and $30 million
- Investment company advisers are always federally registered
- File form ADV and appropriate fees
- Effective after Administrator notification, no later than noon of the 30th day; expires December 31

Investment Adviser Exemptions:
- No office in state and communications directed to 5 or fewer individual residents of the state in 12 months

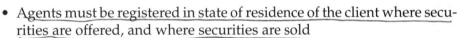

- No office in state and clients are institutions, broker/dealers, or investment advisers only

Investment Adviser Recordkeeping:

- All specific customer and investment adviser records kept for 5 years; must be kept in investment adviser's office for the first 2 years

Broker/Dealer Recordkeeping:

- Same as investment adviser except 3 years instead of 5 years

Class

B/d – 3 yr records ✓

I/A = 5 yrs record ✓

Securities HotSheet

Investment Contract (Howey Decision):	• Investment of money • Common enterprise • Expectation of profits • Solely from efforts of others
Nonexempt Security:	• Must register
Issuer:	• Company, government, or government subdivision that offers or proposes to offer securities
Nonissuer:	• Secondary market transaction • Proceeds do not go to issuer
Primary Offering:	• Initial public offering and any subsequent offering of new securities
Methods of Registration:	• Coordination, qualification
Notice Filing:	• Federal covered investment company securities—file documents with states
Exempt Security:	• No registration under USA required • Look at who the issuer is • Still subject to antifraud provisions
Exempt Transaction:	• Transaction need not be registered under USA • Look at who the purchaser is or how the trade is made

Unethical Business Practices HotSheet

Practices Prohibited of All Securities Professionals:
- Misleading or untrue statements
- Failure to state material facts
- Use of insider information
- Unsuitable transactions
- Market manipulation (pegging, front running, wash sales, matched purchases)

Other Prohibited Sales Practices:
- Unauthorized third-party trading
- Borrowing money from customers who are not banks, broker/dealers, or lending institutions
- Commingling client funds with those of the agent or the firm
- Failing to follow client instructions
- Exercising discretion without written authority
- Effecting transactions not on the books (selling away)
- Failing to report written complaints
- Guaranteeing against loss
- Failing to inform clients of higher than normal charges
- Misrepresenting customer account status
- Creating misleading trading activity
- Promising undeliverable services
- Unauthorized sharing in customer accounts
- Solicitation of unregistered, nonexempt securities
- Misrepresenting Administrator approval

Unlawful or Unethical Investment Advisory Practices:
- Unsuitable investments
- Unauthorized discretion
- Unauthorized third-party transactions
- Excessive trading
- Commingling funds
- Misrepresentation of material facts
- Nondisclosure of information sources
- Excessive fees
- Conflicts of interest
- Unauthorized custody of customer funds
- Operating without advisory contracts
- Performance-based compensation, when legally permitted
- Failing to disclose material legal action in past 10 years at least 48 hours before contracting with client
- Failing to disclose principal or agent capacity

The Administrative Provisions of the USA HotSheet

USA as Model Legislation:
- USA is not *actual* but *model* legislation for each state's own legislation

NSMIA of 1996:
- Eliminates state and federal registration duplication

Securities Litigation Uniform Standards Act (1998):
- Class actions governed by federal standards

Federal Covered Securities:
- Covered by national, not state, regulation
- Includes securities listed on US exchanges, Nasdaq National Market (not SmallCap), issued by investment companies, or sold to qualified purchasers
- Includes government and municipal bonds (but not municipal bonds issued within that state)

Administrator:
- State official responsible for the implementation of the USA

Powers of the Administrator:
- Make rules and orders
- Conduct investigations and issue subpoenas
- Issue cease and desist orders and seek injunctions
- Deny, suspend, cancel, or revoke registrations

Fraud:
- Willful misrepresentation for unlawful gain

Civil Liabilities:
- Attorney's costs *plus* losses on investment *plus* interest minus any income received

Rescission:
- Right to rescind a transaction in violation of the USA—30 day letter

Criminal Penalties:
- Fines or imprisonment, or both

Statute of Limitations:
- Time limits for bringing suit in a case
- **Civil**—3 years from date of sale or of rendering of advice or 2 years after discovering violation, whichever occurs first
- **Criminal**—5 years after date of the transaction